Gang
Intelligence
Manual

Gang Intelligence Manual

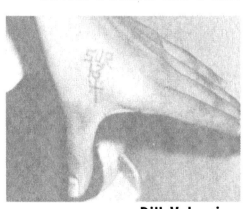

Identifying and Understanding Modern-Day Violent Gangs in the United States

Bill Valentine

Paladin Press
Boulder, Colorado

Also by Bill Valentine:
Gangs and Their Tattoos: Identifying Gangbangers on the Street and in Prison

NOTE: This work is not an official publication of the Nevada State Prisons. The views expressed herein are those of the author and do not represent the position of the Nevada Department of Prisons

Gang Intelligence Manual:
Identifying and Understanding Modern-Day
Violent Gangs in the United States
by Bill Valentine

Copyright © 1995 by Bill Valentine

ISBN 10: 0-87364-844-7
ISBN 13: 978-0-87364-844-8
Printed in the United States of America

Published by Paladin Press, a division of
Paladin Enterprises, Inc.,
Gunbarrel Tech Center
7077 Winchester Circle
Boulder, Colorado 80301 USA
+1.303.443.7250

Direct inquiries and/or orders to the above address.

Visit our Web site at www.paladin-press.com

Contents

Acknowledgments

THIS MANUAL COULD NOT HAVE BEEN WRITTEN WITHOUT THE HELP OF many active criminal justice professionals. Their help is greatly appreciated. I would like to thank them at this time: Correctional Officer Robert Schober, a very talented artist who unselfishly gave his time and talent to draw the hand signs, many of the tattoo patterns, biker jackets, and other sketches; Correctional Officer Catarino Escobar, with whom I spent many hours in the barrios tracking the progress of the gangs through their graffiti and through interviews with active gang bangers, some of whom were victims of gunfire and others who were the perpetrators; Correctional Officer Gary Hill, who has a natural gift for drawing out information from gang members, but who at times let his audacity lead us into situations I was not quite sure we would come out of. I would also like to extend my appreciation to Correctional Officer Michael Cruse, Correctional Officer Glenda Gamble, Correctional Officer Virginia McBean, Correctional Lieutenant Charles Muller, Senior Correctional Officer Walt Rose, and Correctional Officer James Withey. Many others contributed and then vanished. To them I express my deepest thanks.

A special thank you goes to my wife, Jessie, for all her patience and understanding.

Introduction

FOR MANY YEARS, EVERY LARGE CITY AND MANY OF THE SMALLER cities in the United States have been fighting a losing battle against marauding street gangs. Multiple diverse programs have been tried in an attempt to combat the problem, but nothing seems to work. Fifteen years ago, the Los Angeles Police Department (LAPD) came up with a plan it thought would crush the gangs once and for all: Community Resources Against Street Hoodlums (CRASH). About the same time, the Los Angeles Sheriff's Department (LASD) introduced its plan: Operation Safe Streets (OSS).

Both plans were well thought-out; millions of dollars were invested, select officers were given specialized training, and problem areas of the city were placed under a microscope. Radio cars, "rollers" to the teenage gang bangers, rousted the populace, gathered intelligence, made significant arrests, and busted many heads in the process. By the time South Central Los Angeles exploded following the trial of the police officers involved in the Rodney King incident, it was apparent that the city's gang suppression efforts had failed. The main instigators of the riots were identified as street hoodlums—Crips and Bloods.

Not only had the gangs multiplied more than tenfold during the 15 years Los Angeles had been squeezing them, they had also established branch and regional bases in many major U.S.

cities. The Rollin' 60s, one of the largest and most violent of South-Central's Crip sets, were openly dealing crack cocaine in New Orleans, Kansas City, and other cities far removed from Los Angeles. And drug trafficking was only one of their illegal activities. Armed robbery, weapons, mayhem, and murder-for-hire were some of their other endeavors. The only bright spot visible to the law-abiding citizens was that the newly arrived gangsters and the local hoods ripped off and shot up each other in their self-seeking pursuits.

In Los Angeles, when things got too hot, the Crips and Bloods could take refuge in their own "hoods." But in these unfamiliar cities, where they were regarded as intruders, there was no safety zone. Often, when they came under fire thrown at them by the local gang bangers, they were grateful to see the cops show up. After all, if they were arrested, they could use—and abuse—the highest laws in the nation in their defense. But if they were taken prisoner by the local drug dealers, their trial would be swift, their punishment exact, and few of the solid citizens cared much when one street gangster took out another. After all, was it really a crime to kill and rob a drug trafficker?

The L.A. boys, nevertheless, continued their advancement. Soon, in cities like Portland and Seattle, the Crips and Bloods became firmly entrenched. Yet in other cities, street gangs fought them off. In the Bay Area of Northern California, the Los Angeles "posses" met firm and bloody resistance. In Oakland, the Black Guerrilla Family shot and killed Crips and Bloods on sight. In San Francisco, the Sunnydale gang, the Hunter's Point gang, the Dolf Street Nightmares, and other homegrown rowdies did the same thing.

Other older, established gangs with vision could now glimpse the enormous profits to be made by copying the Crips and Bloods. Fixed, turf-oriented gangs ventured out into unfamiliar territory. California prison gangs began moving out past the high walls and gun towers surrounding the prisons to establish beachheads in wealthy, sun-drenched California cities. The violent Aryan Brotherhood (AB), a murderous white supremacist California prison gang, was now issuing orders to the streets for "hits" (murders), drug deals, gunrunning, robberies, and other crimes. The Mexican Mafia (MM), long a California prison gang, became the primary organized criminal enterprise in the East Los Angeles area, and in the Northern California cities, La Nuestra Familia was doing the same thing. The Black Guerrilla Family (BGF), a violent prison gang that has been around for decades, was calling most of the shots in the East Bay area.

The prison gangs that were expanding their operations to the streets had a history of extreme violence, inner discipline, a structured chain of command, and proven hard-core membership. The members, by and large, were brutal, hardened criminals who had earned their place in their chosen gang by virtue of the "blood-in-and-blood-out" code of conduct, in which the prospect is required to commit an act of violence against whomever the gang leaders choose in order to "earn his bones." They had associates doing time in state prisons all across the country and in the federal prison system as well.

The Aryan Brotherhood and the Mexican Mafia had a long-standing alliance honoring each others' hit-lists and working together in crime. La Nuestra Familia had the same arrangement with the Black Guerrilla Family. These factions were sworn enemies, and whether in prison or on the streets, when opposing members came face-to-face with each other, blood would flow. The vendettas born in prison could last a lifetime. And tragically, these prison-bred gangsters were looked up to and served as role models for many street kids just breaking out of the cocoon of puberty.

Too many youngsters growing up in the inner cities looked up to these muscle-bound, tattooed killers and longed to emulate them. These kids had no aspirations to get a high school diploma or go to college. They looked forward to following their dads, their uncles, and their homies to prison. Since infancy, many watched the older men go off to prison and return years later as muscled, tattooed, captivating storytellers. The children would listen for hours as the returned cons smoked, drank beer, and exchanged lies. Growing up in this environment, they had little chance to earn a college degree. Most longed to experience the life behind bars. Any reader who doubts this is encouraged to pick up a copy of *Teen Angel* magazine. Published in Rialto, California, it prints photos of active prison and street gangs and gang members. And despite its high price ($7 to $8 a copy), it is highly cherished by its readers. The pages are abundant with photos of "dressed down" (wearing gang clothing and colors) gang members throwing up hand signs, showing off their weapons and tattoos, and issuing challenges to opposing gangs by their *placa* (graffiti). Many of the photos include infants dressed as gang members in close proximity to the gangs' weapons.

My first exposure to gangs was in the greater Los Angeles area during the 1960s, when I was a member of an ambulance crew. At that time, the gang members fought mostly with chains, knives, baseball bats, and zip guns. Even so, casualties could be brutal. I learned then how to identify gang members and, more importantly, how to relate to them and predict their behavior. Respect—or lack of it—was responsible for countless episodes of bloodshed. Few gangs back then fought over enormous drug profits as they do today. It was all about respect or turf or even shoe shine stands. After 15 years of this work, I embarked on a second career as a correctional officer at Nevada State Prison (NSP).

In my 18 years with the prison system, I have worked face-to-face with inmates daily. For the past five years, I have been assigned to identifying and tracking all suspected gang members in the prison. I watched the Aryan Warriors (AWs) rise from a struggling birth in the 1970s and die a contorted death in the 1980s. I saw the Black Warriors (BWs) grow and fade, only to be replaced by the contemporary Crips and Bloods. Twenty years ago, a prison worker could not identify more than five Hispanic inmates on the yard; today the Hispanics are the group with the most potential for structure and violence. They still fight over respect and turf.

I am a Nevada Peace Officers Standards and Training (POST) certified Field Training Officer and have compiled more than 300 hours of gang intelligence training at various seminars. I am a member of the Nevada Gang Investigator's Association, the Northern California Gang Investigator's Association, the National Major Gang Task Force, and the American Society of Law Enforcement Trainers.

This *Gang Intelligence Manual* contains updated material that was gathered and compiled by active law enforcement and correctional personnel whose daily responsibilities require them to directly supervise many active gang members. Many times throughout the book, I use Nevada and California gangs as examples because these are the gangs with which I have the most experience. Until now, much of the information contained herein has been available only to criminal justice professionals.

I believe that the problem of illegal street and prison gangs is a national epidemic and can only be solved by a combined effort of all citizens. This manual is meant to be used by the professional as well as the layperson as a reference in identifying and tracking illicit gang members. I will gladly exchange information with others on this same trail. Your critique is welcomed.

Bill Valentine
c/o Paladin Press
PO Box 1307
Boulder, CO 80306

Gangs in General

WHAT IS AN ILLEGAL STREET OR PRISON GANG? A GROUP OF PERSONS who share a common belief and associate on a regular basis is not considered to be a gang unless other criminal elements are present, mainly illegal activity. Simply stated, an illegal gang is a group of individuals who meet on a continuing basis to commit illegal acts. If this is happening, then other elements will also be present: leaders or leadership and perhaps a structure of rank within the gang will emerge. But above all, if the gang is active, it will leave a trail of victims, some of who will come forward and inform.

GANG IDENTIFIERS

Gang members often share a common style of dress or wear certain colors or other identifying signs, such as tattoos. They may also post graffiti in their neighborhoods, housing units, or on their literature and mail. Photos may show them throwing up hand signs.

Tattoos
If any single indicator identifies a gang banger it is the tattoo. Gang tattoos are permanent brands that can be understood only by the informed investigator and other gang bangers. Most gang tattoos will be of only one color: dark

blue. Crude ink and needle tattoos done on the street are found along with finely etched prison tattoos depicting myriad designs. The workmanship, shading, and detail may be excellent, especially if done in prison. Names and hometown depicted in Old English script may be found on the banger's back or abdomen. Lettering may be found on the knuckles, arms, neck, or just about anywhere else on the body.

Graffiti

To the casual observer, graffiti would seem to be no more than senseless scribbling. However, to the informed, the messages spray-painted onto the wall contain challenges, counterchallenges, insults, gang roll calls, and the identification of the ruling gang.

Montello Street gang *placa*. This "tag," MTLst, written in large block letters, serves to announce that this turf is claimed by the Montello Street gang, a Hispanic gang. Whoever did the graffiti also spray-painted the names of two rival gangs in the lower right-hand corner of the wall and then added cross-outs or *puto* marks. These are signs of disrespect and a warning to enemy gangs to stay out of Montello territory.

This graffiti is an example of how a gang may challenge others through the use of a "community billboard." The Big Top Locos is the gang responsible. Their *placa* or tag, BTLs, has been "tossed up" on the wall. The phrase *"y-que putos"* means "and so what, queers?" This is a degrading phrase and a challenge directed at all gang members who are not Big Top Locos. The XIII below the *placa* stands for the numeral 13. (The significance of this will be discussed in Chapter 2.)

All or nearly all gang members are known to each other by their monikers, or nicknames. These monikers are part of a gang member's sense of pride and can be seen thrown up with other graffiti on a wall or fence, printed on the bill of an upturned baseball cap, and even tattooed on the body. Monikers are usually given to the gang member by his family, friends, or other gang members. The name is usually given because of an outstanding feature, for example, "Frog" because the person resembles a frog, "Horse Head," "Shorty," "Gimpy," "Pretty Boy," or because of a peculiarity, for example, "Sleepy," "Hungry," "Happy," *"Payaso"* (clown), or *"Bromista"* (joker). The uninformed, however, are cautioned against calling a gang member by his moniker unless they are well acquainted with him. A stranger's addressing a gang member by his moniker can be perceived as an insult or a sign of disrespect.

Drawings

The graffiti artist of a gang is usually selected by the other gang members because he has a talent for the design and placement of graffiti. This illustrator may also have a talent for doing gang drawings. Gang drawings can reveal much about a gang member's thoughts. The astute gang investigator should learn not only how to read graffiti but gang drawings as well.

The drawing on this page was done by a black gang member in prison. It tells a story. This original pasteup was confiscated in a prison shakedown. It was a true pasteup— the three figures were drawn and colored on separate paper using blue ink (to indicate Crip), and then cut out and pasted on the background. The inmate who toiled on the

This sketch was confiscated from a member of the black gang South Side Village Gangster Crips from Pomona, California. It contains many obscure messages.

project was from the South Side Village Gangster Crips in Pomona, California.

The following is a list of elements present in this particular gang drawing and their corresponding meanings:

- *Dog Face Figures*: Black gang members refer to other "down for the set," hard-core gang bangers as dogs. Used in this context, it is a sign of respect—doggedness.

- *Hand Signs*: The two standing figures are shaking hands and flashing gang hand signs. The one on the left is flashing a V for village, and the one on the right is flashing a C for Crip.

- *Sunglasses*: All three are wearing "locs," dark sunglasses. Loc is a term from the Spanish *loco*, meaning crazy. This term is also used extensively by black and Hispanic gang bangers to indicate a person who has courage and will do crazy things without worrying about the consequences. When dressed down, this person will wear very dark, wraparound sunglasses. It is also spelled "lok" by Blood gang members to avoid using the letter C which refers to their enemies—the Crips.

- *Saggin' Pants*: The pants of all three figures are saggin', worn low on the hips, which is another gang member identifier.

- *Gang Logo*: The initials SSV and S are tattooed on the two standing figures. The letters SS and S are stenciled on their pants. This identifies the South Side Village Gangster Crips (SSVGC) from Pomona, California. The kneeling figure has a tattoo on his right upper arm that reads 3X BK. The 3X announces that the SSVGC is a Third World set, an autonomous entity set apart from other mainstream Crips. (As a result, the SSVGC are at war with other Crip sets in Los Angeles.) The BK stands for Blood Killer.

- *Flying Colors*: All three figures have blue (in the original illustration) bandannas hanging from their rear pockets; a pervasive Crip identifier.

- *Enemies*: The kneeling figure is beside the letter N etched into the sidewalk. This N stands for north, and since these three gang bangers are from the south side, it is apparent that there is an enemy set to the north of their hood.

- *Identity Concealment*: The figure shooting the gun has his face covered with a blue bandanna.

- *Beer Bottle*: The beer bottle inside the paper sack is probably a 40-ounce size, which is popular with gang bangers.

Hand Signs

Each gang adopts its own specific hand signs as a means of nonverbal communication. These signs are formed by positioning the fingers and hands to depict letters, numbers, and words. They run the gamut from a simple toss using one hand to a sequence of tosses involving both hands.

I have been amazed watching the dexterity of these gang members in identifying their own sets using their hands and fingers. The ease with which they fashion the complicated signs has always been a source of fascination to me when I've watched former street gang members greet each other in a prison setting.

Hand signs serve to identify the gang, issue warnings, and challenge other gang members. Though in use today, hand signs are by no means a recent phenomenon. Thousands of years ago, Chinese secret societies used hand signs to communicate.

One of the things taught to new recruits by structured gangs such as the Aryan Brotherhood is the sign language of the hearing impaired. This has obvious advantages within a prison setting.

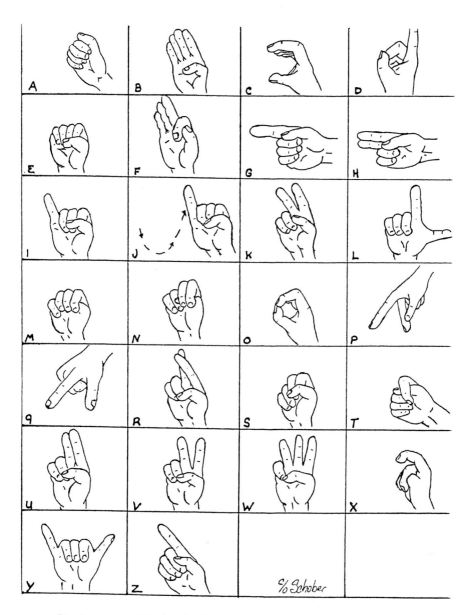

Sign language of the hearing impaired is used by certain gangs, including the Aryan Brotherhood.

Many of the gang hand signs are simple and require only limited flashing of the hand. Others are quite complicated and require several sequential movements involving the use of both hands. The average person catching sight of a gang member throwing up his set may have no idea of its meaning. However, to another gang member, it is unmistakable.

The hand signs identified in this book are typical of those in use by today's gang bangers, but hundreds more exist. Many that have been identified in other reports have been omitted here to avoid redundancy.

Many hand signs you see here may be the same as those of other gangs with the same initials. For example, among the Hispanics, V most often indicates varrio, as in VHLH (Varrio Henderson Los Hermanos from Henderson, Nevada). However, it may stand for something else entirely, as in LV (Lil Valley, one of the older Los Angeles area street gangs).

WHY JOIN?

Why do youths join gangs? The reasons are complex and the answers vary depending upon the point of view of the person answering the question.

Among blacks, it appears the lack of a positive male role model in the home may be the single most significant factor. Quick monetary gain is another. Rap superheroes must also bear some of the responsibility for luring youngsters into gangs.

Among Hispanics, turf, peer pressure, and the all-important machismo may actually be more significant than the acquisition of illegal money.

However, one factor crops up repeatedly when researching motives of prospective gang members: once the prospect has been "jumped in"—an initiation ceremony in which he is required to demonstrate his courage and fighting ability—he attains membership and gains acceptance. This may very well be the first time in his life that the youth has been accepted for what he is. He may now be ready to lay down his life or face the possibility of doing time in order to uphold the tenets of the gang.

In interviewing active gang members, I learned that few of them have any fear of going to prison. In fact, many stated that since they were children, they had looked forward to prison much the same way other youngsters plan for college. Many of these juveniles, since early childhood, have seen their relatives come and go through the criminal justice revolving doors and now eagerly await their turn. Most inmates returning on parole or expiration of sentence entertain the folks back home with stories of how they managed to beat the system through early release, parole, or many other methods.

CASE STUDY: RENO YOUTH GANGS

Reno, Nevada, provides a good example of how youth gangs emerge in a mid-sized city. Ten years ago, gang activity was nearly nonexistent. Today, gang fights, assaults, graffiti, drive-by shootings and other gang crime is common. Innocent people, including infants, are sometimes caught up in the crossfire between warring gangs. Unfortunately for the law-abiding Hispanic community in Reno, an unusually large number of those arrested in connection with gang-related crimes have Latino names.

The first indication of the arrival of gangs in Reno was the appearance of graffiti throughout the city. That was soon followed by gang crime and other acts of violence that were traced to local ganged-up rowdies. What fueled this phenomenon? In a high percentage of cases, experienced gang members moved here from larger cities with their families to get away from other gangs. These newcomers brought gang sophistication with them and, in many instances, became the catalysts for the emergence of gangs in their newly adopted city.

Four such youths came to Reno from Los Angeles, where they were members of the 118th Street East Coast Crips. It wasn't long before they were schooling the local youngsters in Reno on how to be successful gang bangers. They continued their big city ways in Reno until they got caught up in the gang rape and robbery of a 13-year-old girl. The four were subsequently identified by the victim, arrested, tried, convicted, and given lengthy prison sentences.

The media are also responsible for the expansion of these gangs. In too many instances, the attention they give to gangs and gang members acts as a magnet that lures other youngsters into the gang scene. After the movie *Colors* was released, authorities in cities all across the country noted an increase in gang activity. When the movie was shown in California, shootouts between Crips and Bloods erupted right inside the movie theaters. A few years ago, the Reno Police Department adopted a policy of not giving out the gang name to the media after a gang crime having noted that doing so tended to increase gang activity.

Some of the street gangs in Reno have appeared briefly and then vanished, such as the Gizmos and the Tijuanitos (TJs). An El Salvadoran and his cousin attempted to form a street gang patterned after Los Carnales (CXL) of Los Angeles a few years ago in the Neil Road area. The gang probably never had more than half a dozen hard-core members, and the El Salvadoran soon ended up in a Nevada prison. (He has since been released and is being closely watched by local law enforcement.) Others that have remained intact despite a shaky structure and dubious leadership include:

Montello Street (MTLst)—Latino
Big Top Locos (BTL)—Latino
Lewis Street Locos (LST)—Latino
Maravillas (MVR)—Latino
Neil Road Vatos (VNR)—Latino
South Side Locos (SSL)—Latino
Sunset Locos (SST)—Latino
Eastwood Tokers (EWT)—Latino (Carson City)

118th Street, East Coast Crips—Black
E. Second Street Bloods—Native American
Tongan Crip Gang (TCG)—South Sea Islanders
Supreme White Power (SWP)—White
White Aryan Resistance (WAR)—White
War Skins (Skinheads)—White
Skinheads Against Racial Prejudice (SHARP)—White

Most of the active gang bangers in the Reno area are unskilled high school dropouts. They stake out and claim their turf through the use of graffiti. In many cases, the turf they claim may be nothing more than an overcrowded apartment building in a run-down neighborhood. Yet they consider the territory theirs and will instantly challenge an outsider if he looks like he doesn't belong.

"*De donde eres?*" This benign question asks, "Where are you from?" However, when used by gang bangers, it becomes a blunt challenge—"What gang are you from?" The active gang banger looks upon others of his age and race as other gang bangers, so when he directs this question to a stranger in the neighborhood, he may suspect the newcomer of being a member of a rival gang. If the outsider cannot come up with a believable response, he may quickly end up a statistic.

2 ▶ Hispanic Gangs

MEXICAN AND CHICANO YOUTH GANGS HAVE EXISTED IN THE UNITED States for at least the last 80 years, bound together by culture, tradition, a sense of identity with family and neighborhood, and loyalty. In some of the older, established gangs on the West Coast, it is not unusual to learn that three generations of the same family have gone through life as members of the same gang. The early gangs—and others that followed—formed along geographical lines, taking their names from landmarks within the area, such as the White Fence gang, the Temple Street gang, and the Maravillas of Los Angeles.

Many of these early gangs can trace their roots to the beginning of this century when Mexican immigrants streamed across the border, fleeing from the civil unrest and abject poverty. The people, for the most part, were hard-working, simple peasants entering a strange country where anti-Mexican sentiment was widespread. (Many Americans were all too aware of the atrocities committed against U.S. nationals living in Mexico by Pancho Villa and his band of rebels, not to mention their bloody incursions across the border into the United States.)

Yet the immigrants continued to pour into this country. Few could speak the language. Many were targets of predators on both sides of the border and sought refuge here among family and friends and others they could trust. They stayed close together, often living in overcrowded, crudely constructed shacks. Some were able to bargain for existing houses or cabins. Their colonies became known as "barrios," from the Spanish word meaning suburbs. When not working the fields, they stayed close to home—within their barrio—where they could relax, drink a few beers, and enjoy their new existence. After all, those lucky enough to find jobs were now making more money than ever before, and not only were they saving some, they also had the means to care for the legions of newborns—all U.S. citizens by right of birth—now swelling the ranks of the barrios.

As the number of immigrants entering the United States multiplied, so did the number of settlements. Immigrants from the same area or town in Mexico tended to gather together in the United States, forming their own barrios. Hence, many of the barrios took on their own character and personality and were distinguished from the others not only by their locations but by the names their residents gave them.

Inevitably, disagreements broke out between residents of different barrios. Brawls followed, some of which undoubtedly escalated into prolonged feuds. Eventually, a dweller of one barrio who had made enemies in another could only venture into unfamiliar turf at some risk. Of course, these barrios were still in their infancy and provided shelter to a large number of transients at any given time, but it was expected that new arrivals would reinforce the efforts of those immigrants living in each particular barrio.

This is one way long-standing gangs in cities such as Los Angeles, Tucson, San Antonio, Albuquerque, and other cities bordering Mexico became established. Thousands of others along the way were born, developed, and passed into oblivion.

SUREÑOS Y NORTEÑOS

Frequently, gang *placa* and tattoos of prison and street gang members will contain the words or numbers *sur*, *sureño*, 13 or *norte*, *norteño*, 14.

Sureños

"*Sur*" is the Spanish word meaning "south." "*Sureño*" literally means "one from the south" or "southerner." When these terms are used in Hispanic graffiti, they refer to Southern California.

Also, the number 13, as used by the Hispanics, is synonymous with Sur and Sureño and also indicates the gang's origin in Southern California. There are several reasons for this. Approximately three decades ago, when Hispanics in the California prisons began organizing into gangs, the Mexican Mafia gang recruits were, for the most part, inmates from the Los Angeles area. The Mexican Mafia was also referred to as *La Eme*, which is Spanish for the letter M. Since the letter M is the thirteenth letter of the alphabet, the Mexican Mafia members used the number 13 synonymously with the letter M. Also, the area code around the Los Angeles area is 213,

The graffiti on this apartment building in Carson City, Nevada, identifies the gang members who claim that turf as being from Southern California.

which again supports the number 13. As more Mexican nationals get involved in gang activity in this country, the use of Sur–13 as a reference to their Mexican origin increases. Sureño graffiti can also be found frequently in many cities deep inside Mexico.

In Hispanic graffiti, the number 13 may be written in several ways: 13 (Arabic numerals), X3 (combining Roman and Arabic numerals), XIII (Roman numerals only), *trece* (Spanish for 13), or 3'ce (a combination of Arabic numerals and abbreviated Spanish).

Regardless of how the number 13 appears within a gang's *placa*, the meaning is the same—the gang traces its origin, or allegiance, to the Southern California area and considers as its enemies the "Norteños," or "14s," from Northern California. In addition to having "Norteño" enemies, the gang may also be at war with many other barrios that claim to be Sureños like themselves.

Norteños

The Hispanic street gangs in Northern California (north is usually conceded to be all of California north of Bakersfield) number in the hundreds. Graffiti can be found in nearly every northern city, and gang activity is rampant. The gangs may have as few as five or six members or hundreds. These gangs fight black, Asian, white, and other Hispanic gangs.

Most of these Northern California gangs claim to be *norteños*, or northerners, and as such claim (declare membership of) *catorce*, or 14, referring to the fourteenth letter of the alphabet, N. Fourteen is usually written as 14 (Arabic numerals), XIV (Roman numerals), or X4 (a combination of Arabic and Roman numerals).

The Norteños have been at war with the Sureños for decades, both on the streets and inside the prisons. Curiously, even though the majority of the Northern California gangs claim to be Norteños—and as such regard the Sureños as the common enemy—many of the Norteño gangs war against each other.

When spray-painting their graffiti, the Northern California gangsters will usually include a reference to their place of origin with the word Norte or Norteño, the letter N or the Spanish equivalent *ene*, or the number 14.

Sur–13 and Norte–14 as Generic Terms

One important fact to remember: when you see street gang graffiti that contains either the Sur–13 or Norte–14 designation, bear in mind that these are generic terms only. There are hundreds of active Sureño gangs that regard each other as enemies, just as there are Norteño gangs that do. However, when the active gang bangers get to prison, it is customary for the Sureños to group together, just as it is for the Norteños to do so. In California, the dividing line that separates the two is generally considered to be Bakersfield. However, it is not uncommon to see 13 graffiti in the north as well as 14 in the south. Identification of the "players" (participants) can be accomplished by carefully examining their tattoos, literature, photos, graffiti, clothing, and associates.

Many will readily reveal their gang affiliation out of their sense of pride; others will out of fear of being housed with enemy gangsters.

HISPANIC GANGS IN RENO

Northern Nevada is beginning to see a multitude of Hispanic gangs, some in the formative stages and others well established. Many of these gangs are enemies with the other local gangs, yet almost all of them claim *trece* or 13.

The Wedekind Road Area

The Wedekind Road area, composed of high-density apartments, has been the scene of shootings and violence. It is known to the police as a high-crime gang-infested neighborhood. Gang bangers, dressed down, stroll the sidewalks in groups or just hang out. Older model cars, dented and held together by variously colored panels, cruise the streets. Gang graffiti dots the area.

The Montellos are probably the largest and most active Latino gang in Reno. They claim the area of Wedekind Road and Montello Street in northeast Reno. Their ranks are filled with the youths of Mexican and other Central American immigrants and Chicanos—American-born youths of Hispanic parents. They actively recruit new members and accept youths of other nationalities, such as blacks, whites, Asians, and South Sea Islanders. Many of their members are doing time in Nevada prisons, including one who professes to be an OG (original gangster) and founder of the gang. Their *placa*, MTLst, can be seen throughout the area.

Occasionally, members of nearby street gangs venture into Montello turf to cross out Montello *placas* and throw up their own. When on a mission, these intruders are usually armed, oftentimes high, and ready to challenge the local gang bangers. Many times they bring their women along to carry and conceal the weapons. If pulled over by the police, there is a good chance the women will not be subjected to a search. Another trick they use is to cut a hole in the floor-boards of their "rides" and use the opening to dump their weapons and drugs if pulled over by the police. A floor mat usually covers the opening.

The Montello gang members have been feuding with other gangs for quite some time. Blood has been shed during their clashes with the Big Top Locos, the Maravillas, the Tijuanitos, and others. Most of these fights have been over turf or machismo. Many brawls have "jumped off" (erupted) because a rival gang has slipped into Montello turf at night and spray-painted its own *placa* on a wall or other conspicuous place as a challenge. When this happens in turf claimed by another gang, the ruling gang must accept the challenge or lose face. When members of these rival gangs run into each other in town or while driving on the streets, a bloody clash may follow.

In the photo on page 25, the Big Top Locos have spray-painted their *placa* on a retaining wall on Wedekind Road.

The Big Top Locos are primarily a Los Angeles gang from the west side. They also go by the name West Los. They now have a chapter in Reno. This is a sample of their graffiti.

The large block letters are well done, stylized, and shaded, which is consistent with good Hispanic graffiti. (An accomplished graffiti artist in a large city may spend years perfecting his skills. In addition to being the gang's artisan, his talents may also be in demand within the legitimate sectors of the barrio painting wall murals. When he comes to a much smaller city with less gang sophistication, his work will be recognized.) When this quality of graffiti appears, it usually means gang bangers from California or other states have come into Reno and hooked up with the local rowdies. Since this area is within the boundaries of the Montello barrio, it is obvious that the BTLs have issued a challenge, which must now be dealt with by the Montellos.

The Big Top Locos are one of the chief rivals of the Montellos, and both gangs have suffered casualties when the two have crossed paths. On one occasion, a 15-year-old who was hooked up with the BTLs went out with two other teenagers looking for Montello gang members. When they saw a carload of suspected Montellos, they pulled alongside the car and the youth fired six shots from a .22-caliber gun into the enemy car. Unfortunately, one of the rounds smashed into the head of a youth in the other car, wounding him critically. The youngster who did the shooting is now in the Nevada State Prison.

The Maravillas

The Maravillas claim the area near Morrill Avenue and 6th Street. Their turf is well staked out. It is alleged that they are into heavy drug dealing. Many of their leaders come from the state of Guererro in Mexico, where they have a reputation for settling their disputes using machetes. They have had many confrontations with the Montellos. The Maravillas may be affiliated with other gangs of the Maravilla district in Los Angeles County, which is home to some of the oldest Hispanic gangs on the West Coast. The word *maravillas* means "wonders" or "marvels" in Spanish. In the photo on this page, the tag MVR #1 Sur 13 has been spray-painted on

The Maravillas are one of the oldest gangs in Los Angeles. They are engaged in a long-standing feud with the Montellos. This graffiti was found in Reno and serves as evidence that they have a chapter there.

a wall. This tag proclaims to all that the Maravillas are number one and that their point of origin is Southern California.

IDENTIFICATION OF HISPANIC GANG MEMBERS

Confirmation of Hispanic gang members is made on the basis of many identifiers. Ideally, at least three of these identifiers should be present when confirmation is required.

Race
Most are of Latino origin; however whites, blacks, and others such as South Sea Islanders can also be found.

Age
The ages of Hispanic gang bangers will run a broad spectrum from the peewees, who may be as young as 9 or 10 years old, on up through the *veteranos*, who may be in their

50s. Most Hispanic gang members, however, range in age from the early teens up through the 20s.

Clothing

Most Hispanic gang members favor dark athletic clothing, but not only that with the Los Angeles Raiders logo, as has been widely reported. Other athletic gear is just as popular, especially black clothing with the Chicago Bulls or San Jose Sharks logos.

When a gang member has lost a homey in a drive-by shooting or other violent act, the surviving members of the gang may honor him by displaying on their shirts and jackets, "In memory of . . ." or the Spanish equivalent, "*En memoria de . . .*" Frequently, pictures of the slain member reproduced by computer will adorn their clothing.

Pants and Shirts

Oversized pants, sagging at the waist and with the cuffs rolled up, are common. Dickies brand overalls, with the shoulder straps hanging down, are popular, as are creased jeans. A favorite color combination is black and white—black baggy pegged pants and a white shirt that may be a button dress shirt or a sleeveless or sleeved T-shirt. Many T-shirts can be bought with gang-oriented screen printing. Oversized Pendleton shirts, buttoned at the neck and worn outside the pants, are an old-time favorite.

Hats

Dark watch caps are still seen frequently, as are baseball style caps, which are either worn backwards or with the bill turned up above the forehead. The gang name, moniker, or messages such as 187, R.I.P., etc., may be visible on the upturned brim. UNLV (University of Nevada at Las Vegas), when seen on a Northern Structure (NS) gang banger's upturned cap bill, stands for "Us Norteños Love Violence."

Bandannas, Moco Rags

These are either hanging from a rear pocket or worn covering the top of the head and tied in back. They may also be worn as a sweatband. *Moco* (Spanish for mucus) rags may be seen in a variety of colors; however blue is the identifying color of the Sureños and red is the color for the Norteños. Black is seen also, especially at funerals.

Shoes

Athletic shoes are preferred, such as Nike, Fila, Converse, and other popular brands. Another gang identifier is shoes worn with different colored laces (for example, black shoes with white laces, white shoes with black laces, blue or red laces on white shoes, etc.). Some bangers like to use two pairs of laces per shoe, one white and one black. The laces may spell out an abbreviation or gang name, such as CXL, XIV, or X3. Also, graffiti may be stenciled or inked onto the shoe.

Coats

During the winter, large black parkas are common, many with logos. Navy P-coats and trench coats are also popular. Most of the clothing will be oversized. This makes it easier to conceal weapons and gives the wearer a more sinister look.

Colors

As stated above, the Sureños identify with the color blue, the Norteños with red. The Border Brothers, gang members who have immigrated here from Mexico and other Central American countries, identify with the color black. Of course, there are variations of this color code. Specific gangs may decide on an entirely different color.

Tattoos

One of the first tattoos a Hispanic gang banger may get is three dots that signify "*mi vida loca*" (my crazy life). This tattoo may be on any part of the body, but usually it is seen on the hand, fingers, face, or neck.

The Pachuco cross may also be one of the first tattoos an Hispanic gang banger may get. During WWII, street brawls erupted between uniformed servicemen and Hispanics in Los Angeles. The Hispanics called themselves *Pachucos*, lawless street gang members of Mexican ancestry. Their distinctive tattoo was a Pachuco cross—a cross worn on the web of the hand with three evenly spaced rays radiating upward. The Chicanos who wear the tatto today are, in effect, "hitching a ride" on the street brawlers of yesterday. Another common tattoo is the teardrop under the eye.

Legends about these tattoos abound. "The cross means he killed a cop." "The cross means he murdered a rival gang member." "The unshaded teardrop means he did a drive-by shooting; the shaded teardrop means he killed a rival during a

A three-dot tattoo such as the one on this gang banger's face signifies the saying "*mi vida loca*" (my crazy life).

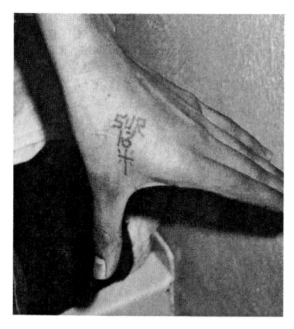

The Pachuco cross is often found tattooed on the web of the hand. Note that above the cross is the number 13 and "Sur," indicating that this gang banger is a Sureño, a southerner.

The teardrop tattoo is usually found on the skin under the eye.

drive-by." "The teardrop means he did five years in the joint." The fact is that nearly every Hispanic youngster growing up in a gang environment will get one of these tattoos early in his career—it certainly is no confirmation that he has killed a cop or done time in the joint. There is no single interpretation for these tattoos, only what the wearer would have you believe.

Many youngsters entering prison for the first time wearing these tattoos are scared to death of what could happen to them if challenged by someone who has known prison as home for years and who, in fact, may have entered prison long before the youngster was born. The truth, when known, will probably be that he got these tattoos on the street in hopes of impressing others like himself. Inside he has to prove himself, and tattoos are not enough.

Somewhere on his body, the gang member may have his barrio tattooed. It could be on his fingers, on the web of his hand, or even on his forehead. A city name may be displayed in large block letters on the banger's abdomen or upper back. Gangsters are proud of where they're from, and many go to great lengths to advertise it.

A favorite place on the gang banger's skin to show off his nickname, or moniker, is on the side of the neck. Smiley, Silent, Payaso, and Loco are all common monikers.

Other Hispanic Tattoos

Midwestern and eastern U.S. Hispanics are making their way west and are becoming conspicuous on the streets and within prisons. They ran with street gangs back home that had names such as Latin Kings, Latin Jivers, and Spanish Cobras. In general, these three Hispanic gangs are subsets from two large enemy gangs: the People Nation and the Folks Nation (see Chapter 4). The tattoos they bring with them are the six-point star of the Folks Nation and the five-point star of the People Nation. The Latin Kings wear a five-point crown tattoo that also has the letters L and K, one on either side of the crown. The hometown may also be indicated using letters, such as NY for New York.

Hand Signs

Hand signing to identify gang members, having started in China, is a relatively recent development in the West. Its practice seems to have gained popularity in the United States with the inception of the black gangs, the Crips and Bloods. The Hispanics have also adopted this means of nonverbal communication.

Generic hand signs usually require little or no imagination, such as those for Sureño and Norteño. However, most gangs identify their particular set or *cliqua* in a much more

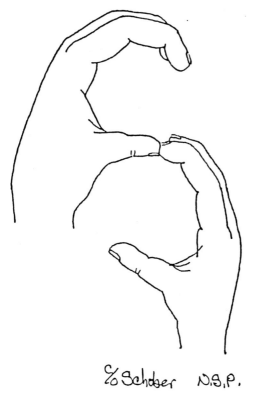

Here both hands fashion the letter S, which indicates "one from the south" or "a southerner." This is a favorite symbol used by Hispanic gangsters from Southern California to distinguish themselves from the gangsters to the north.

S

sophisticated way. In some cases, identification of the set or *cliqua* requires several successive movements of the hands.

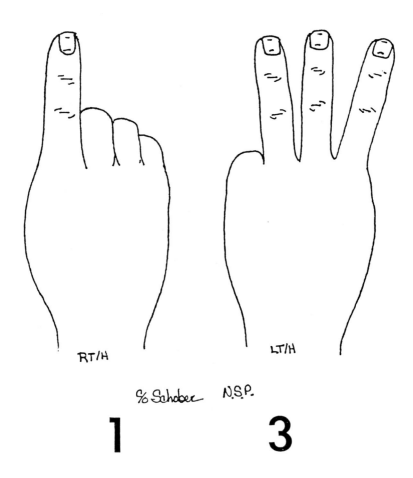

RT/H   LT/H

1   3

The number 13, a reference to Southern California, is seen consistently in Hispanic gang graffiti, tattoos, and literature.

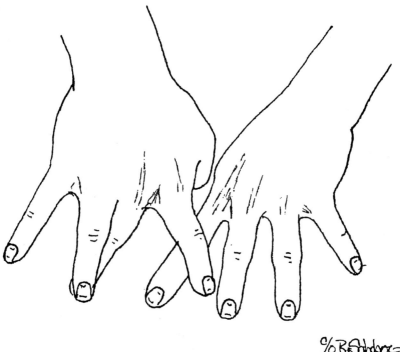

M XIII

The M identifies the Montellos in Reno, and the Roman numeral XIII identifies the Montellos as a gang claiming to be Sureños—having roots in Southern California.

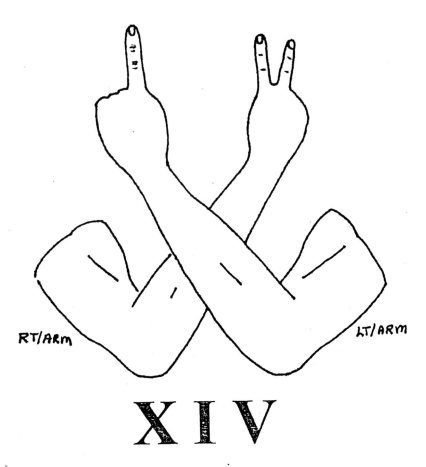

RT/ARm

LT/ARM

XIV

The number 14 refers to the fourteenth letter of the alphabet, N, which is used extensively by the Nuestra Familia (NF) (see chapter on prison gangs) and Northern Structure gang members in Northern California and within the California prison system. Here, both hands and arms are used to fashion the Roman numeral XIV.

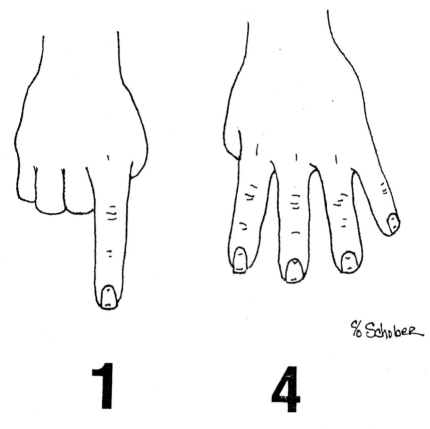

1   **4**

This is another way Nuestra Familia and Northern Structure gang members flash the number 14.

Writing

The sample of Hispanic gang writing on page 38 was found crumpled on the ground near Woodside Drive in Carson City not long after a young gang member was shot and killed by a rival. It is considered to be an excellent example of Hispanic gang writing because of the stylized letters and words, the correct spelling, and the context of the story.

Although some black gang writing is similar to this style,

= EAST SIDE) STORY) =

THERE IS A WONDERFUL
PLACE ON THE EAST SIDE
WHERE LOVERS GO TO SHARE)
THE MOMENT ON THE EAST
WHEN YOU FELL IN LOVE
THIS IS THE PLACE)
WHEN TWO COME TOGETHER
THEY MEET A ROAD TO
HAPPINESS AND LOVE
THE ROAD SAYS ENTER
THE MAGIC WORLD THEY ENTER
        "AND KILL"
THE ROAD MOVES EM TO THE
        "EAST SIDE"
THEY WERE EVEN HAPPIER
BUT AS THEY LOOK BACK
THEY JUST SAY OH IT'S
        TWO GANGSTERS
          IN LOVE)
BUT THEN WE WENT ON TO
THE REAL WORLD AND WE
KEPT SAYIN I HAVE TO
        EAST SIDE)
WE ARE DOWN FOR WHATEVER)

                SENIOR BANGER
                    "91"

This sample of Hispanic gang writing was found crumpled on the ground near Woodside Drive in Carson City. It was probably written by a member of the neighborhood's local Hispanic gang, called the Eastwood Tokers.

Translation:
There is a wonderful
Place on the East Side
Where lovers go to share
The moment on the East
When you fall in love
This is the place
When two come together
They meet a door to
Happiness and love
The door says enter
The magic word they enter
"Sur XIII"
The door opened to the
"East Side"
They were even happier
But as they look back
They just say oh it's
Two gangsters
In love
But then we went on to
The real world and we
Kept sayin thanx to
East Side
We are down for Woodside.

this can be identified as Hispanic gang writing because none of the Bs or Cs have been crossed out. If this piece were written by either a Crip or Blood, one of these letters would be crossed out wherever it appeared.

The other validation is in the wording, "We are down for Woodside," which means the unknown author is "down for" (active with) the local Hispanic gang which claims Woodside Drive as their turf—the Eastwood Tokers.

HISPANIC GANG TERMINOLOGY

Hispanic gang terminology incorporates a mixture of both English and Spanish words. Many of these words are slang and are understood only by the gang members. This spoken mixture is known as "calo." For example, the Spanish word *ganga* means sale or bargain. When used in street Spanish, it can mean literally "gang." The word police can be indicated by "*aguas con la jura*," "*placa*," "*chota*," "*patotas*," "*manotas*," or in better understood Spanish, "*aguas con el policia.*"

Aguas: Careful, watch out.
Aguitado: Mad, furious.
Aguja: Needle.
Aztlan: Occupied Mexico (California, New Mexico, Texas, Arizona, Colorado Treaty of Guadalupe).
Baica: Bike.
Barrio: Neighborhood; gang.
Boina: Watch cap.
Brakas: Brakes.
Caca: Drugs; shit.
Cachuca: Baseball cap.
Califas (Norte–Sur): California (North–South).
Calma: Calm down.
Carcancha: Old junker car.
Carcel: Jail.
Carcos: Shoes.
Carnal: Gang brother.

Carrucha: Car.
Catorce: Fourteen; synonymous with Norte.
Chansa: Chance.
Chante: House, home.
Chavala: Girlfriend, chic.
Chela: Cerveza, beer.
Chingamos: We fuck 'em up.
Chiva: Heroin.
Cholo: Gang member, current generation.
Chota: Police.
Chuco: Veteran gang member.
Clica: Clique, gang.
Condado: County jail.
Controlamos: We control.
Con Safos (C/S): What you do to us, you get back double.
Cuate: Friend.
Culo: Rear end.
Dedo: Finger. (*Poner el dedo*: to point a finger, to blame.)
Eme: The letter M; the Mexican Mafia.
Ene: The letter N; the Northern Structure.
Ene Efe: NF, Nuestra Familia.
Ese: Dude, vato.
Farmero: Farmer, Nuestra Familia gang member.
Firme: Solid person; fine.
Frajar: To light a cigarette.
Frajos: Cigarettes.
Filero-Filo: Knife.
Ganga: Gang.
Gavacho: Anglo.
Gemelo: Twin; best friend.
Hermano De La Frontera: Border Brother.
Hierba: Marijuana.
Huevos: Anglos.
Jalapeño: Any law enforcement officer who wears a green uniform.
Joto: Homosexual.
Jura: Police.

La Llanta: Negro.
La Migra: Immigration.
La Raza: The race (Hispanic).
Manotas: Police.
Maricon: Homosexual.
Mayate: Negro.
Mecha: Match.
Mojado: Wetback.
Morro(a): Dude, *vato*, (girl).
Morrito(a): Young boy, (young girl).
Mota: Marijuana.
Nada: Nothing.
Nester: Nuestra Familia gang member.
Norte: North; usually pertains to Northern California.
Norteño: Northerner; usually pertains to one from Northern California.
Orale: Hey! All right!
Patotas: Police.
Pildoras: Pills.
Pinacates: Negros.
Pinche: Lousy, bloody, no good.
Pinga: Prick.
Pingo: Promiscuous.
Pinta: Prison.
Pintada: Graffiti.
Pinto: Prisoner.
Placa: Gang graffiti; badge, police.
Por Vida (P/V): For life.
Puto: Homosexual.
Quemar: To snitch.
Ranfla: Car.
Rata/Raton: Rat, snitch.
Refla: Food.
Refinar: To eat.
Rifa: Rule, (this gang) rules.
Rifamos: We rule.
Rifan: They rule.

Ruca: Old lady, girlfriend.
Simon: Yes.
Soplon: Snitch, rat.
Sur: South; usually pertains to Southern California.
Sureño: One from the south; a Southern Californian.
Talco: Powder; cocaine.
Tonto: Stupid.
Torcido: Twisted; imprisoned.
Trece: Thirteen; synonymous with Sur.
Trucha: Careful, watch out.
Varrio: Neighborhood; gang.
Vato: Dude; gang member.
Vato Loco: Crazy gang member.
Veterano: Gang veteran.
Vida Loca: Crazy life.
Watchalo: Watch it!
Ya Stuvo: It's over with.
Yesca: Marijuana.
Y'que?: So what? What are you going to do about it? (a challenge)
Zodiaco: Zodiac.

3 ▶ Crips and Bloods

THE CRIPS AND THE BLOODS WERE BORN IN THE GHETTOS OF LOS Angeles. Much has been written about them during the past two decades, so this report gives an overview of what is already well known.

The Crips were the first of the two factions to get the attention of the LAPD. During the late 1960s, violent crime in South Central Los Angeles increased dramatically, and a large proportion of those committing the crimes boasted of being a Crip. Much of this activity occurred on high school campuses.

The LAPD officers working the area conducted field interviews (FIs) in addition to responding to radio calls. Juvenile officers gathered intelligence, and the detective bureau added its input of information regarding the Crips. All incoming data was fed into a central intelligence pool, and soon a predictable profile emerged: the Crips were a new phenomenon in South Central.

The police were well acquainted with other gangs from the neighborhood. The Huns, Slausons, Sir Valiants, Gladiators, and Black Cobras were just a few of the criminal gangs the police had been dealing with for years. These groups engaged in strong armed robberies (in which the robbers use only physical force against the victim, not weapons), purse snatches, gang fights, car thefts, and burglaries. The members were pretty well known to the police working the area, and their criminal activity was predictable. When not engaged in petty crime, these gang members picked up spare change working in car washes, picking up scrap metal, or hustling whitey when he ventured into the area looking for reefer or a woman.

The picture emerging of the Crips was entirely different. The members were younger (many had been expelled from school), antisocial and hostile toward others, cared nothing for life or property, armed, and engaged in all forms of violent criminal activity, ranging from brutal gang beatings to murder. Their victims, for the most part, were residents of their own neighborhoods or youths from other hoods. Other people living in the area, many of who held down jobs, maintained homes, and were trying to recover from the havoc created during the Watts riots of 1964, again became fearful of leaving their homes at night. Crime increased to an all-time high, and the newly arrived Crips were being held responsible, a reputation that didn't cause them any loss of sleep.

The Crips recruited aggressively, especially in and near the local high schools. Many wannabes hung out with Crip gang members and pleaded to join. Before becoming a member, a prospect was sent on a mission, usually an illegal act of violence. If the mission was completed to the satisfaction of the Crip leaders, the prospect was jumped in or "courted in." This rite took many forms, the most common being for the initiate to make his way past a double line of gang members, many with weapons, who would beat him as he proceeded past them on foot. If he showed ample toughness, he was in.

Once in, he belonged. He found acceptance, closeness, sharing of criminal profits, and family. All too many of these gang members were raised in a single parent environment, usually by their mother, who most often was rearing more than one child on whatever she could get from welfare. Stability in the home was unknown. These youths grew up on the streets hustling nickels and dimes and often standing as lookouts in front of the projects, watching for the despised rollers while the older youths peddled bud or stripped cars.

.To increase the Crip membership, other youths were sought out as prospects and pressured to join. They had few choices. If they refused, they were beaten repeatedly, day after day, and whatever money or valuables they had were taken. In the end, they would either have to join or move from the neighborhood. There were no other options. If they continued to resist or brandished a weapon, retaliation was swift and exact. The Crips would have it their way. They were the shot callers in the hood.

Stories as to the origin of the name Crips abound: the name was taken from the movie *Tales from the Crypt*, from a street gang called the Cribs, or from the word Kryptonite, a substance powerful enough to subdue Superman. Or how about this one: one of the original gang members was lame and had to use a cane when walking. One night when he was hanging out with other gang members, the gang spotted a group of elderly Japanese Americans waiting for a bus on Central Avenue. The gang pounced on the Japanese like a pack of coyotes, grabbed purses from the women, and fled into the night. By the time the police arrived, one old lady, trying to give a description of the gang members, kept repeating in broken English "a crip, a crip with a stick." A reporter on the scene picked up the words, and in his story attributed the act to a gang called the Crips.

I was working as an ambulance driver in the Watts, Willowbrook area during the formative years of the Crips. The stories going around at that time were that members of this new gang all carried canes and left their victims crippled, and so became known as Crips.

Another explanation of the name's origin comes from some of the most recently jumped-in Crip members who insist that the name is political: Common Revolution in Progress. This, however, appears to be a definition of the 1990s with no roots. The true origin of the word may be lost forever somewhere within the empty shell casings, blood, and tears long since washed out into the Pacific Ocean.

The structure of the gang appeared to be a spur-of-the-moment thing, with the leadership being assumed by different members depending upon who was present during a criminal act, his status within the gang, and his access to transportation, weapons, and so on.

When on a mission, the Crips got in the habit of covering their faces with a railroad type bandanna, the favorite color being dark blue with white designs. This bandanna could be purchased anywhere and effectively concealed their identities while leaving their eyes uncovered. When not used as a mask, the blue bandanna was folded and hung from a back pocket. This is how the color blue became the official Crip color, and most of the gang's members always had a bandanna or wore an article of blue clothing at all times, whether on a mission or just hanging out. It became a mark of pride, and blacks began killing blacks over a color.

Soon other youths from different neighborhoods, anxious to join the Crips, formed their own Crip chapters or "sets." In Compton, an incorporated city near Watts, a 16-year-old Washington High School student who went by the name of Tookie and a few of his friends started a Crip set and named it the West Side Crips. When members of the West Side Crips encountered Crips from other sets, they regarded each other as family and used the greeting "cousin" or "cuzz." This soon became the accepted greeting shared by all Crips.

After the West Side Crips became firmly established in Compton, other youths from Watts and the adjacent areas began forming their own Crip sets. Some of the early ones were the Rollin' 60s, Hoovers, Main Street Crips, and Grape Street Watts. Scores of others would follow. At this stage of development, the Crip sets all got along well with each other. But trouble was brewing elsewhere.

Other youths, fed up with being pressured by the Crips, formed their own groups with the intention of standing up to the "Blue Rags" and fighting back. The youths living on Piru Street in Compton formed their own gang for self-protection and called themselves Pirus. They, too, decided to use a railroad bandanna to hide their identities and chose one that was red with white designs, thus adopting the color red to set them apart from the enemy Blue Rags'. They also chose to call each other "blood," so they could be identified by their wearing of red and by the way they greeted each other.

Youths in other areas of South Central took note of the way the Pirus had ganged up to defend themselves against the marauding Crips, and before long, other gangs were formed and affiliated with the Pirus. There were now "Red Rags" and "Blue Rags," declared enemies at war against each other. Sometimes the battles erupted spontaneously when chance encounters occurred. Shotguns and pistols replaced knives, razors, and sticks, which were once the weapons of choice in South Central. At times, gang members would "posse up"—meet, get into their cars, and head out with some criminal intent such as a gang fight. The result would be a bloody drive-by shooting. The Bloods, outnumbered by roughly seven to one, soon built up a reputation for savagery in their war against the Crips. And what was just as important, all Bloods joined the fight. Regardless of which set they claimed, the Bloods supported each other. Bounty Hunters, Bishops, Swans, Brims, Blood Fives, or Pirus, they all claimed Blood, and they all joined together in their war against the common enemy, the blue-raggin' Crips. Not so with the Crips. They were developing enemies within their own sets.

Crip Infighting Develops

Sometime early in the 1970s, a girl attending Horace Mann Junior High School was dating a banger who claimed Rollin' 60s. After a spat, she left him and took up with a banger from the 83 (Eight-Tray) Hoover Crips. In the days that followed, bangers from both sets were involved in fist-fights. This problem continued to escalate between members of the two sets until one of the Eight-Tray gangsters shot and killed a Rollin' 60. This started an all-out war between the two sets, in which scores of victims have been shot and killed since the initial skirmish.

Drive-by shootings became frequent in the areas claimed

by the 83 Hoover Crips and the Rollin' 60s. And not just gang bangers were casualties. Innocent persons, including infants, were victims. Small-caliber weapons were given up and replaced by Uzis, AK-47s, and MAC-10s.

Other feuds developed between Crip sets that added to the carnage. The South Side Village Gangster Crips from Pomona claimed to be a Third World set and considered all Crip sets with a name ending in zero to be an enemy. This effectively announced to Crip sets such as the Rollin' 40s, 50s, 60s, etc., that another war had been declared. Now, in addition to fighting the Bloods, more Blue Rag sets were embroiled in a civil war.

New sets were being formed throughout the area, not only within South Central Los Angeles, but within other incorporated cites of Los Angeles County and the unincorporated areas as well. The Imperial Village Crips, Nut Hood Watts Crips, Palmdale Gangster Crips, Venice Shoreline Crips, and Playboy Gangster Crips all claimed blue. The Bloodstone Villains, Lime Hood Pirus, Pacoima Pirus, and Samoan Warriors claimed red. And these were only a sampling.

At this stage of development, the preferred drugs being sold on the streets were marijuana, PCP, cocaine, and heroin. Marijuana was plentiful and affordable, PCP was devastating to the entire area, cocaine was restricted to only those who could afford it, and heroin was for the aficionado. But that was soon to change.

CRACK COCAINE

The cocaine being offered for sale in the inner cities during this time was cocaine hydrochloride (HCL), a refined cocaine that was cut as it passed from supplier to dealer. This effectively reduced its purity to less than 50 percent, which is still a much higher concentration of the drug than today's average of 10 to 20 percent. The usual method of usage was snorting. Before the turn of the century, cocaine was a legal substance that was added to many products such as Coca-

Cola. Catarrh powders, some of which were nearly pure cocaine, were sold as a cure for sinus trouble and headaches, and the suggested method of using them was by snorting.

The cocaine hydrochloride became much in demand in the United States among affluent Americans. What was needed by the enterprising gangster on the street was a cheaper form of cocaine that could be smoked—not snorted—and rewarded the addict with an instantaneous high, a product that would create such an army of addicts, it could be sold on the streets 24 hours a day.

Cocaine is an alkaloid found in the leaves of the coca shrub grown and cultivated in the Andes region of Ecuador, Peru, and Bolivia. The waxy, oval-shaped leaves have been chewed by the local Indians for at least 2,000 years to relieve pain, extend energy, and elevate the mood. The peasants living in these regions depend upon proceeds from the coca leaf cultivation for their livelihoods. And even though the coca leaves are a legal product sold in the open air markets of Bolivia and Peru, the business of growing and harvesting the coca leaves is controlled by the drug lords. They operate with no opposition from the police.

The city of Cochabamba, with a population of 300,000, lies on the western edge of the Chapare, the principal coca-growing region in Bolivia. Cochabamba boasts magnificent high-rise buildings, outstanding restaurants, and exceptional hotels. The city's residents enjoy the highest standard of living in the country. Cochabamba is also the gateway to the Chapare jungle, where the coca leaf is grown and harvested. In the residential area of the city, drug lords have built mansions, and the peasants have the means to enjoy television on color sets that cost as much as most Bolivians living in other parts of the country earn in six months.

Inside hidden processing plants within the Chapare jungle, peasants convert the coca leaf into cocaine hydrochloride, which is then shipped to the United States. In the United States, the cocaine hydrochloride is stepped on—diluted or cut—by the addition of sugars such as lactose, or a neutral substance such as talcum powder, or local anesthetics such as Novocain. This reduces the strength of the cocaine to about 20 percent. However, this is at best an estimate, because when the market shows a glut, the cocaine is usually sold with a higher purity. And during times of high production, it is not uncommon to see tons upon tons of cocaine stockpiled in the jungle awaiting shipment.

In the search for a way to get the drug into the bloodstream more quickly and intensify the high, it was learned that the cocaine base could be freed and isolated from the hydrochloride. This method of freeing the base resulted in a much more concentrated form of the drug with fewer impurities which could be smoked rather than snorted. Sprinkled on a marijuana cigarette and inhaled, the drug entered the bloodstream almost instantly and rewarded the user with a short but intensely powerful feeling of euphoria and omnipotence. The disadvantage was that the freebasing process required the use of highly flammable ether along with a complex apparatus, including acetylene and butane heating torches.

By 1980, somewhere in the neighborhood of 20 percent of cocaine addicts were freebasing their poison. The remainder, not wanting to risk the dangers of freebasing, continued to snort the white crystalline powder. And then on the night of June 9, their caution was upheld when comedian Richard Pryor exploded in flames while freebasing coke. Pryor suffered third-degree burns over his upper body and face. This of course sent Pryor to the hospital for extensive surgery, and the headlines sent an army of addicts on a desperate scavenger hunt looking for a safer method of freebasing.

In many parts of the world, addicts were experimenting with different chemicals to find a less hazardous way of freebasing cocaine. The solution was relatively simple: cooking the HCL in common baking soda, which proved to be a safe and efficient method of "rocking" the cocaine. During the cooking process, the mixture will make cracking sounds, and this is what gave crack its name.

Smoking

Crack cocaine smoking requires the user to have the crack—or rock—and smoking paraphernalia, which includes a glass smoker (a bong), a small wad of steel wool, and a source of heat. The bong is made from glass and has three main parts: the main chamber that holds water as a coolant, the upturned arm that has a screen to hold the crack, and the mouthpiece (see the illustration below). The rock is placed on the screen and heated using a butane lighter or homemade torch fueled by a supply of 150-proof rum. Unlike marijuana or tobacco, the crack does not actually burn. As the heat is applied, the crack begins to vaporize, and it is this heated vapor that contains the cocaine base that is drawn into the lungs. Cocaine base begins to vaporize at 85°F. At this point, the smoker experiences a tremendous euphoric rush that is considered to be the ultimate high. However, it is of short

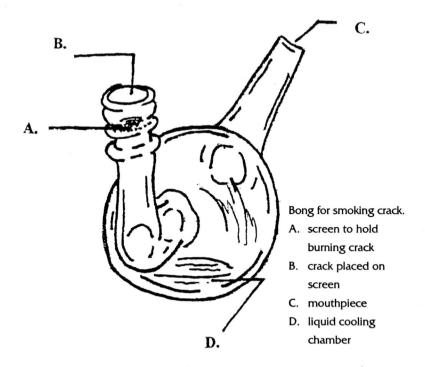

B.

C.

A.

D.

Bong for smoking crack.
A. screen to hold burning crack
B. crack placed on screen
C. mouthpiece
D. liquid cooling chamber

duration, from 15 to 20 minutes, and when it begins to wear off, the smoker crashes into a depressive low. For susceptible persons, addiction follows after only a few hits.

Crack was an instant hit in Los Angeles. The going price for a gram of cocaine powder was around $75. When crack arrived, a rock could be bought for as little as $5. Addicts immediately went for crack. It was cheaper, and the rewards far exceeded those of the white crystalline powder. However, crack was by far the most addictive drug to hit the inner cities. Thousands of new addicts were created every week. And as they continued to smoke, the letdowns became intolerable for many who were feeding their habit during all waking hours.

OVERNIGHT MILLIONAIRES

The Crips and Bloods had been killing each other before the arrival of crack, but crack supplied the incentive for wholesale slaughter. Every neighborhood developed its own network: the addicts (baseheads), the suppliers, the dealers, and all the supporting cast—runners, lookouts, soldiers, and spies. Some of the housing projects developed their own Crip or Blood sets. At night the players came out much like insects. Dealers hawked their wares, lookouts alerted the dealers to the presence of rollers, the soldiers provided armed coverage or went out on patrol and engaged the enemy in bloody skirmishes, and the spies went out on intelligence gathering missions.

Fortunes were made peddling the poison to the endless hordes of addicts screaming for more. Blue Rags and Red Rags, each fighting to protect their own interests, stockpiled weapons and recruited vigorously. Crip sets that had previously gotten along now went to war against each other. The Blood sets continued to support each other and launched a new offensive directed against the Crips. Rapid-fire, high-powered military-type guns were the weapons of choice. Each set fought for the right to be the sole distributor of crack in specific areas. It was all about "clockin' Gs"—making big bucks.

Competition was fierce. Drive-bys became a household word. Peewees, too young to drive, did walk-bys. Blood flowed in the streets; on many weekends there would be nine or ten drug related murders. A few of the more iron fisted climbed out of the street-level carnage to become the crack generation's primeval godfathers.

Brian Bennett, aka Waterhead Bo

When only 24 years old, Bo was arrested at his million-dollar home in Tempe, Arizona. Bo had been dealing directly with the Colombian cartels. He teamed up with Mario Ernesto Villabono-Alvarado, and together they organized a nationwide drug ring operating out of Los Angeles that distributed more than a ton of crack cocaine a week.

Wayne Day

Day, a product of the Watts Varrio Grape Street Crips, became a rich and powerful crime godfather through sales and distribution of crack cocaine. He attempted to unite Crips and Bloods into one powerful organization. At one time he spoke to over 500 gang bangers during a meeting in which he stressed unity and criminal control of all crack cocaine sales. During the meeting, he attempted to instruct the gangsters on such salient facts as drive-by shootings, methods of tying up the police patrols using bogus phone calls, and other disruptive practices.

Michael Harris, aka Harry–O

Harry–O is alleged to be the kingpin behind a criminal enterprise that distributes crack cocaine in California, Arizona, Texas, Michigan, Illinois, Indiana, Iowa, Louisiana, Florida, Missouri, and New York. It is said he deals directly with Mario Villabono-Alvarado, the same as does Waterhead Bo. Harry–O, for a number of years, kept himself well insulated from the law by spreading his vast wealth around and retaining sharp, high-priced lawyers. However, he finally took a fall when he was arrested for the murder of one of his employees. Sentenced to 28 years in prison, Harry–O continued to run his criminal activities from within his San Quentin prison cell and dabbled in legitimate business endeavors, including the financing of Broadway shows with proceeds from his drug trafficking network.

SPREAD OF THE OCTOPUS

Other fast-paced U.S. cities had been screaming for rock cocaine, as had a myriad of small towns with names no one had ever heard of. They wouldn't have to wait too long. The Rollin' 60s were one of the first Crip sets to respond. The 60s dispatched scouts from Los Angeles to assess the situation in other cities. The reports that came back were encouraging: a $10 or $20 rock in Los Angeles could be sold in St. Louis for $50—a handsome markup.

The Rollin' 60s followed up the initial scouting reports by sending out heavily armed soldiers to establish beachheads in cities like Sacramento, Las Vegas, Wichita, Dallas, Denver, and others. Crack sales soared.

Methodically, distribution networks were established and franchises were offered. Local gangs were given the option of accepting a crack-house franchise or going to war with the invading Rollin' 60s from Los Angeles. Many accepted the franchise. Others didn't.

Some of the cities invaded by the 60s had their own long-established gangs and weren't about to submit to the intrusion. The Los Angeles boys were met in San Francisco by the Hunter's Point gang, the Sunnydale gang, Deuce Town, and others, and were warned to leave. Apparently, the 60s sensed they were outgunned because they heeded the warning and left town. In Oakland, the same thing happened when they confronted the violent prison and street gang the Black Guerrilla Family. In the midwest, the Black Gangster Disciples, the Vice Lords, El Rukns, and others repelled the invaders at their borders and sent them back to Los Angeles. However, in the cities that offered little resistance, the Rollin' 60s became firmly entrenched.

In Los Angeles, crack cocaine became the drug of choice for the disadvantaged youths of the inner cities. And the Rollin' 60s gang bangers expanded their criminal activities to include armed robbery, extortion, weapons sales, auto theft, and murder-for-hire.

Las Vegas Joins the Crack Age

Las Vegas was ready. Already home to many illegal street gangs, especially in Northtown, Las Vegas' gangs welcomed the opportunity to expand and become part of the lucrative crack cocaine supply chain. The Donna Street Crips (DSC), Gerson Park Kingsmen (GPK), Undercover Crips (UCC), White Street Mob (WSM), Northtown Gangsters (NTG), and other Crip sets opened their arms to the Rollin' 60s from Los Angeles.

Bloods in Las Vegas that had been fighting the Crips were the Playboys (PB), West Coast Bloods (WCB), Pirus, and Hoods. As in Los Angeles after the introduction of crack cocaine, the Crips and Bloods went after each other with a renewed vengeance. All gang bangers smelled the enormous profits to be made; they all wanted to become rich crack dealers. They became dealers, but few got rich. In fact, most became increasingly poor, despite skyrocketing sales. Those selling crack became crack addicts themselves and sold just to support their own destructive habits.

Drug dealer rip-offs and killings became routine. Crack addicts went to where the source was. If it meant killing a crack dealer, so be it. Some of the populace questioned whether or not killing a crack dealer was actually a crime.

Las Vegas became a miniature Los Angeles. Drive-bys were a nightly occurrence. Blood flowed and crime increased at an alarming rate. Bloods and Crips fought in the streets with high-powered guns. Children and babies were occasionally caught in the crossfire. As in Los Angeles, the Bloods got along with each other, but the Crips developed infighting feuds; the Donna Street Crips fought with the Vegas Rollin' 60s, and the Gerson Park Kingsmen had bloody encounters with other Crip sets. The youths of Northtown were "bangin' and slangin'," not in an effort to make a lot of money, but just to be able to buy enough crack to support their own habit. When the money wasn't there, drug dealers were ripped off, shot, and killed.

Kluckheads (addicts) would do whatever was necessary to stay high. Some girls were known as "toss-ups" or "strawberries"—addicts that traded sex for crack. It became difficult to find anyone in Northtown who hadn't lost a relative or friend in the incessant drug war.

Many bangers went on missions downtown or on the strip. Hotel guests were beaten and robbed; some were killed. Hotel rooms were ransacked. Gamblers leaving casinos were mugged. Car theft reached an all-time high. The police were forced to add additional officers for patrol and many times came under small-arms fire when investigating reports in Northtown. A new Clark County detention facility was built at the cost of millions of dollars and became overcrowded not long after completion. A new prison in Ely was opened and filled to capacity. Another one in Lovelock was built and then left vacant due to lack of staffing funds. Governor Bob Miller worked hard to get gang suppression laws passed that would keep gang members in prison for longer periods. Still the gangs flourished, and many times while in court during trial, gang members were disruptive, flashed gang signs to their homies sitting among the spectators, and broke out in laughter—even while looking at a life sentence. At times it seemed as if the whole world had lost its values; to many, crack cocaine was all that mattered.

Back in Los Angeles

In Los Angeles, rock houses had become fortresses with reinforced walls, barred windows, and steel doors with gun ports that looked out past 6-foot-tall cyclone fences. Electronic surveillance cameras scanned the yards and streets. Inside, the dope dealers received the currency, and then slipped the crack back to the addict through slots in the walls that were guarded by shooters. The LAPD mobilized squads of riot-equipped police to smash the rock houses. It became necessary to convert an armored personnel carrier into a mobile battering ram with a 14-foot steel beam. When a rock house was shattered, so was business, but only temporarily. The next day a new location was chosen, and the cycle repeated.

Los Angeles Crips and Bloods could now be found in cities across the United States. Seattle and Portland had declared parts of their cities to be battlegrounds after the Nine-Deuce Hoovers from Los Angeles moved in. The Eight-Tray Hoovers had taken over other cities, as had the 118th East Coast Crips, so named because their hood was east of the Harbor Freeway. Rollin' 60s graffiti could be found on tenement walls in Kansas City and New Orleans.

By the time the 1980s had come to a close, the LAPD and the LASD had been at war against the Crips and Bloods for over 10 years. In fact, 10 years earlier the LAPD had formed CRASH and the LASD had formed OSS in an effort to stem the tide of gang violence. Now there were more gangs than ever and violence was at an all-time high. Estimates as to the number of active gang bangers in the Los Angeles area ran as high as 100,000. Rap superstars were making millions rapping about bangin' and slangin' and killing cops.

By 1990, the Los Angeles gangs had extended their tentacles eastward. And simultaneously, the Jamaican Posses had begun their migration to the west. Caught between the pincers were the midwestern states, such as Illinois and Missouri. It wouldn't be an easy incursion for the advance guard. Chicago and the adjacent areas had their own brand of killers. The El Rukns, the Black Gangster Disciples (BGD), the Vice Lords, and the Spanish Cobras were only a few. Another emerging gang to be reckoned with out of the ghettos of south Chicago was the Brothers of the Struggle (BOS) (discussed in Chapter 4).

UNITY

Rodney King, a black California prison parolee, was on everybody's mind after an amateur video photographer taped him being beaten by several Los Angeles policemen using PR-24 batons. Civil rights activists, the American Civil Liberties Union (ACLU), and the National Association for the Advancement of Colored People (NAACP) followed the sequence of events in the aftermath of the incident, including the trial of the policemen in Simi Valley in 1992.

When the policemen were subsequently acquitted of the serious charges against them, South Central Los Angeles became an inferno. Again, as during the Watts riots decades earlier, the inner-city denizens torched and looted their own neighborhood. Scores were killed and many more were left maimed and crippled. Property damage was in the hundreds of millions.

The Crips and Bloods, already seasoned veterans of bloody street battles, viewed this new uprising as a means to further their own criminal tendencies to rob, plunder, and loot the neighborhood stores. Others, caught up in the moment, pulled victims from their stalled vehicles and beat them senseless.

In the aftermath, a noticeable change had settled over the enemy gang members. They began to label themselves as blameless victims—not the brutal street hoodlums they actually were. And they developed a following who agreed with them! Past vows of retaliation against each other were laid aside by both Crips and Bloods. Cries of unity echoed throughout South Central. Blue and Red spoke of merging. Meetings were held. Plans were laid. Drive-by shootings slowed in the hood. One could now see Crips and Bloods partying together in parks that were once reserved solely for the Red or Blue bangers that claimed the turf. The police were targeted by the Crips and Bloods gang banging together.

Las Vegas

This idea quickly spread to Las Vegas, where the Crips and Bloods had been ripping off and shooting up each other. Suddenly, Northtown gang bangers stepped up their attack against the police. Calls would come in to the switchboard and when the radio cars pulled up looking for the scene, shots would ring out, causing the patrolmen to seek cover until backup arrived.

And it wasn't just the police; civilians who ventured into the area, especially at night, became the targets of the rampant gang members that were now terrorizing the area under the umbrella of the newly acquired truce.

Nazi Termination Squad

On August 11, 1991, 18-year-old Robert Colleen, an alleged skinhead, went after a black youth suspected of stealing a bicycle. When Colleen cornered the young man and struck him with a bat, the black youth pulled out a gun and shot Colleen to death. During the autopsy, the pathologist noted a tattoo on Colleen's wrist with the initials CIS.

A year later, the black youth was tried in district court for murder. This was about the same time the truce movement was gaining momentum in Las Vegas. During the trial, it was revealed that the CIS tattoo on the dead youth's wrist stood for "Christian Identity Skins." Many of the Northtown black gang bangers that had been shooting each other now became caught up in the idea of being skinhead killers and refocused their gun sights.

A new unified gang set started tagging the North Las Vegas area calling itself Nazi Termination Squad (NTS). This gang purports to be operating in Las Vegas and is out to kill skinheads, or Nazis. As of this writing, little has been heard from this new set. They may be for real, or it may be just another passing fancy. Already, reliable sources have said the truce is falling apart. One poignant observation of the tag, though, is that the words are all spelled correctly, which is sometimes unusual with rampaging high school dropout gang bangers.

This photo depicts the NTS tag on a Las Vegas block wall with a crossed-out swastika, the word "unity," a crossed-out "KKK," and a crossed-out "CIS." The inference to be drawn here is that the NTS intends to unify and go after members of the KKK and the CIS. Note that the N in the tag NTC (Northtown Chapter) is crossed out. This is done because the word Nazi starts with the letter N.

IDENTIFICATION OF CRIPS

Race

Members are predominately black, although the Crips will accept whites into their sets under unusual circumstances. Occasionally, the whites who live in the neighborhood want to join a local gang and are willing to submit to the initiation rites. Hispanics are also admitted; There is one Crip set in Los Angeles with a mixed membership that calls itself Los Partners Crips.

Symbols, Graffiti, Tattoos

The name and logo of the gang are used liberally in their graffiti and tattoos. The gang banger's moniker is spread

Here the name of a local gang banger, Boxer, was thrown up on a fence. It was then crossed out by an enemy and a large "187" was thrown up to the right of the name. The meaning here is clear—Boxer has offended someone and is now marked for murder.

around as well. Other symbols seen frequently are 187 (the California penal code for murder) and BK (Blood Killer).

The use of the words Cuz, Cuzz, Crip, Krip, and the letter C all indicate Crip. Logos such as a clump of grapes are used by the Grape Street Crips (Watts Varrio Grape, Grape Street Watts) in their graffiti and tattoos. Similar indicators are used by other sets. Crips refer to Bloods as slobs, and this is also seen in their graffiti.

As a general rule, black gang graffiti is less stylized and lacks the polish seen in Hispanic graffiti. However, it is every bit as pervasive; the gang bangers tag the area, and the authorities cover it up. Back and forth. It becomes a community problem of considerable expense.

Clothing
501 Levi's or Dickies pants, blue wool Pendleton shirts, and Nike or Converse jogging shoes are in style, as are British Knights jogging shoes, whose logo sends a message (BK, Blood Killer).

This graffiti depicts a Crip holding a smoking shotgun. Note the word "KRIPS" to the figure's left side and the phrase, "Fuccin Slob Killa."

Some of the Crip graffiti is nothing more than scribbling, lacking style and polish. This graffiti identifies the Donna Street Crips from Las Vegas.

The Crip gang banger likes to wear his Levi's or Dickies sagging and his shirt buttoned only at the top (this allows him to conceal his weapons but have quick retrieval when necessary). A railroad type blue bandanna is a must, either hanging from his rear pocket or used in covering his face when he wants to conceal his identity. Watch caps and baseball caps worn backwards or with the bill turned up are preferred head coverings. Team jackets with the Los Angeles Raiders, Chicago Bulls, or San Jose Sharks logos are a favorite. Levi's jackets are still in vogue.

Hair
Jerri curls, corn rows, fades, and styles with the wearer's nickname or gang name cut into the hair are popular. Since styles continue to change, different designs are seen from time to time.

This drawing done by prison inmates depicts two Crip gang bangers gunning down an enemy Blood. Both Crips are wearing blue clothing that exhibits a BK logo. The gangster on the left is shooting a shotgun, and the one on the right is using an Uzi. The gangs identified are the Rollin' 30s, 60s, 90s, and 100s. Note also the street sign, "BK Street."

Colors

Blue is the recognized color of the Crips, although it is not the only color worn. Grape Street Watts Crips identify with the color purple. The Gerson Park Kingsmen, a Las Vegas Crip set, identify with the colors black and green—signifying a black nation with green money. The Comstock 40 Boys, another Las Vegas Crip set, identify with the color brown and always carry a brown bandanna. Their name is derived from their habit of drinking beer from a 40-ounce bottle. The Donna Street Crips, also from Las Vegas, identify with dark blue, while their enemies to the west, the Rollin' 60s, prefer light blue.

Hand Signs

Black gang members often refer to showing hand signs as "flashing." The black gangs were the first U.S. gangs to incorporate flashing as a means of identification. As more sets developed, each came up with its own hand sign. When passing an ally, these gang members would "throw up their set" (flash their sign) as a greeting. This worked well until many of the sets began fighting each other over turf and drug sales.

When a black gang member flashed an enemy, it was taken as a direct challenge and fights and shooting followed. This trend continues today. During drive-by shootings, those in the car shout their gang name, or name and number, at the enemy gang, flash their hand signs, and roar away in a cloud of gunpowder and exhaust.

The hand sign may also be used to show respect during the funeral of a dead gang member. As the homies pass by the coffin to pay their last respects, they may flash the gang hand sign for the deceased to "see."

Many Crip and Blood sets identify with a number as well as a gang set name. For example, the Gerson Park Kingsmen identify with the numbers 3-6-9. The Playboys, a Las Vegas Blood set, identify with the numbers 3-5-7. The Donna Street Crips identify with the numbers 3-4-7. The numbers are the street numbers on housing projects where the gang members are from.

Writing

The piece of writing on page 71 is a gang roll call for Crip sets. A roll call is a roster listing the names of all members. "Slob," the Crip name for Blood, is crossed out, as is "Piru," the name of the original Blood gang from Piru Street in Compton, California. The entire message says "Slob Killa, Piru

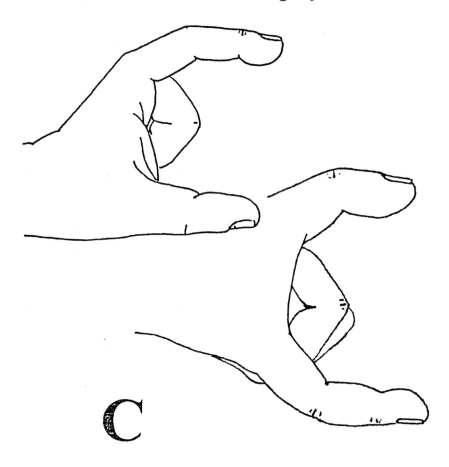

This is a generic flash meaning Crip. This gesture identifies the gangster as a Crip without identifying the particular set.

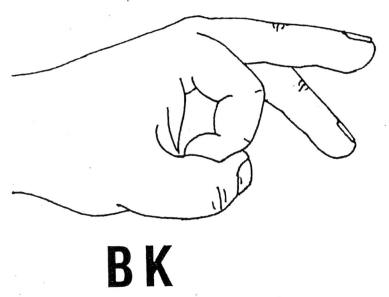

B K

This is another generic flash used by Crips meaning Blood Killer.

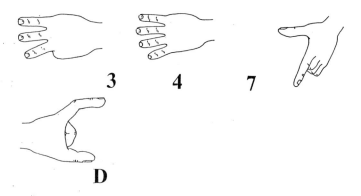

The hand sign for the Donna Street Crips involves throwing up a trey-four-seven followed by a D.

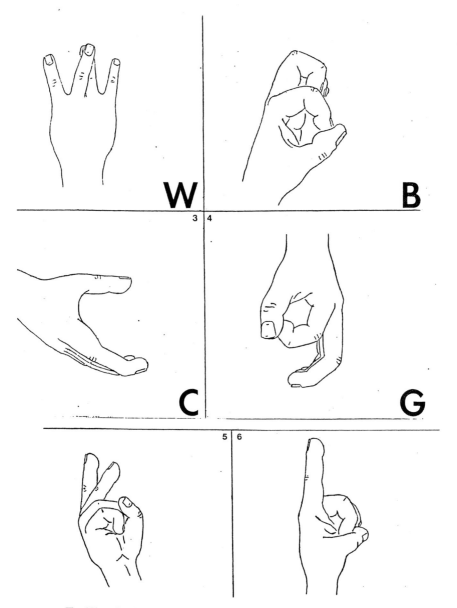

W

B

3 | 4

C

G

5 | 6

The West Boulevard Crip Gang of Los Angeles also goes by the name "The Deuces." Throwing up their hand sign requires the use of both hands. A short version is done by throwing up the "deuces" and then the forefinger indicating "number 1."

to." Perhaps in error, the architect of this piece neglected to cross out all the Bs and Ps (shame on him).

IDENTIFICATION OF BLOODS

All the identifiers that apply to the Crips also apply to the Bloods, with one or two exceptions. The Bloods identify with the color red, and they shy away from the letter C. For example, a cigarette becomes a bigarette, and Compton becomes Bompton. When they must use the letter C, it is crossed out. The Bloods refer to the Crips as Crabs.

The roll call on the following page is for the United Crip Gang (UCG) in Compton, California. It was confiscated by police. "ES" preceding the gang name indicates it's from the East Side, "WS" means it's from the West Side.

Translation:

ES Grape Street Watts
ES Hat Gang Watts
ES Holme Street Watts
ES Front Street Watts
ES Bacc Street Crip
ES Holme Town Crip
ES Beach Town Mafia
ES Insane Crip Gang
ES Blvd Mafia Crip
ES Rollin Twenty Crip
WS Eight Tray Gangster
ES Nut Hood Watts
ES PJ Watts
ES Ten Line Gangster
ES Fudge Town Mafia
ES Play Boy Hoo Ride

ES Foe Duce Gangster
WS Ghost Town Crip
WS Dod Rocc Crip
WS Altadena Blocc Crip
ES Lynwood N Hood
WS Imperial Village Crip
WS Broadway Gangster
WS West Coast Crip
WS Water Gate Crip
ES Miccenly Crip
WS Deker Park Crip
ES East Side Fortey
WS Cat Wall Crip
ES Avalon Garden Crip
WS Mafia Crip Gang
ES Euclid Blocc Crip

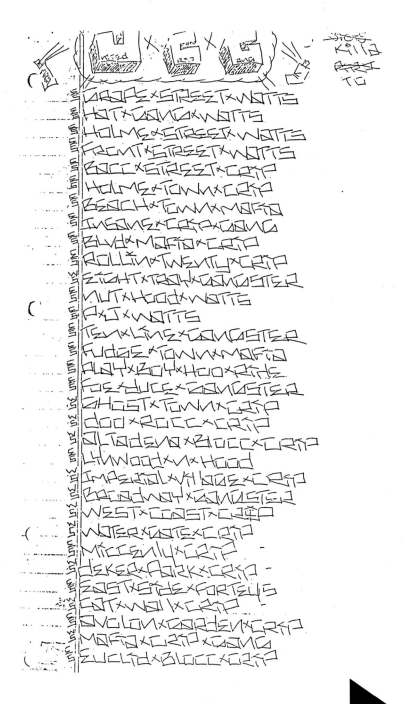

Colors

There are a few variations to the color code of the Bloods, the most obvious being practiced by the Lime Hood Pirus. The Lime Hood Piru gang members always wear an article of green clothing along with the red. For example, a red shirt and shoes and a green jacket, green pants and a red shirt, red jogging shoes with green laces, or maybe a red shirt and a green cap.

Hand Signs

The Bloods also use hand signs as a means of identification, pride, and respect. The first Blood hand sign was a "P" to represent Piru Street, where the first Blood gang originated. As their ranks grew, other sets developed out of the original Piru set. These sets maintained close friendships with the original Pirus, but each developed its own hand sign for identification.

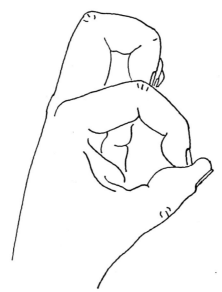

This hand sign forms a capital B for Blood—a universal Blood gang hand sign.

Blood

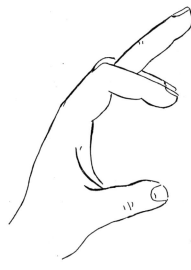

This hand sign meaning "Crip killer" is a popular Blood greeting.

C K

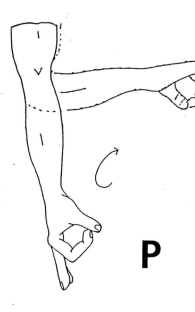

The hand sign for the Pirus, a Las Vegas Blood set. In Compton, California, the Pirus were the first Bloods to organize into a viable gang in order to defend the area against the newly formed marauding Crips.

P

P B

This is the hand sign for a Las Vegas Blood set called the Playboys. They throw up their set using one hand to fashion the Playboy bunny's ears.

BLACK STREET GANG TERMINOLOGY

A and B Conversation, C Your Way Out of It: Stay out of my business.
Against the Curb: Broke, no money; smoked out on crack.
AK: AK-47 rifle.
Baller: Blood name for gang member making money.
Ballin': Having more money than others.
Bangin': Gang banging.
Basehead: Cocaine addict.
Bay Bay Kids: Unkempt children.
Beemer: BMW auto.
Benzo: Mercedes Benz.

Bo: Marijuana.
Bomb: Hit song.
Boned Out: Ran away, chickened out.
Book: Leave, run off.
Breakdown: Shotgun.
Bucket: Old, beat up car.
Bud: Marijuana.
Bullet: One year in jail or prison.
Bumper Kit: Girl's butt.
Bumpin': Lookin' good.
Bumpin' Titties: Fighting.
Bussin': Shooting at someone.
Buster: Phoney gang member.
Buzzed: Drunk, high.
Caine (Ice Cream, Product, Flavor, Work, Ya-O, Snow Balls, Candy): Cocaine.
Cappin': Shooting someone.
Car Hop: A girl who wants you just for your car.
Chillin' (Kickin' It): Getting together with friends and chatting, joking, laughing, having a drink, etc.
Cluckhead: Crack cocaine addict.
Crab: Blood name for Crip.
Crippin': Crip gang banging.
Crossover: Hook up with a different gang.
Crumbs: Tiny bits of rock cocaine.
Curb Serving: Selling crack on the corner.
Custer: Phoney gang member.
The Cut: A popular song.
Cuzz: Crip greeting.
Dead President: Money.
Dead Rag: Red Rag, Blood.
Deep: Many.
Deuce-Five: .25-caliber handgun.
Dis': Disrespect.
Do a Ghost: Leave, run off.
Doggin': Treating someone bad.
Dope: Sounds good, great.

Double-Deuce: .22-caliber handgun.
Down for Mine: Able to fight well.
Down for the Set: Loyal to his set, will fight to protect it.
Drama: Confrontation.
Draped: Wearing a lot of gold jewelry.
Drop a Dime: Snitch on someone.
Dumpin': Finish selling the dope.
Durag: Bandana covering the head.
Endo: Marijuana cigarette.
Ends: Money.
Essay: Mexican/Chicano.
Faded: Disrespect.
Fades: Styled haircuts, designs showing on the sides.
Fifty Rock: Fifty-dollar piece of rock cocaine.
Flaggin'/Flashin': Throwing gang signs, gestures.
Fly: Good-looking girl.
Forty: 40-ounce beer bottle.
Four-Five: .45-caliber handgun.
Frog: Girl with few morals.
Gat: Gun.
Gauge: Shotgun.
Gee'd Up: Gangstered up; dressed in gangster style.
Get Down: Fight.
Ghetto Bird: Helicopter.
Ghetto Star: Top-notch gang banger; gang leader.
Good Drag: Good conversation.
G-Ride: Gangster ride; stolen car.
Grip: Having money; trying to get money.
G-Star: Gangster.
Gucci: Looking good in clothes.
Hat Up: Leave.
Head Hunter: Girl who turns tricks for money or drugs.
Head Up: Start a fight.
High Beams On: High on cocaine.
High Roller: One who's making a lot of money.
Hit: If you're smoking, others want to join you.
Ho: Whore.

Homes/Homie: Fellow gang member.

Hoochie: Low-life female.

Hood: Neighborhood.

Hoo Rah: Loud talking.

Hoopty: Car.

Hubba: Crack cocaine.

Hubba Pigeon: Addict picking up bits of crack from the ground.

In the Mix: Involved in gang activity.

Jackin': Taking something by force.

Jam: Confront.

Jimmy Hat: Condom.

Kite: Prison letter.

Kluckhead: Crack cocaine addict.

Knockin' the Boots: Romantic relationship.

Loc: Crazy, tough, down for the set, *loco*; also refers to the dark wraparound sunglasses worn by this person.

Lok: Blood spelling for the word loc.

Lookin': Looking for drugs.

Main Man: Best friend; backup

Mark: Banger who has no loyalty to his gang; he crosses over whenever he can benefit.

Mission: A gang assignment.

Mobbing: Homies hanging out.

Mobile: Large rock of crack.

Mud Duck: Ugly girl.

Nine: Handgun.

Off Brands: Enemy sets.

O.G.: Original gangster; older member of the set.

On the Pipe: Smoking crack.

One Time: Police.

Player: Pimp, hustler, not a gang member.

Poo Butt: Sissy.

Proper: Sounds good, it's right.

Props: Respect.

Put in Check: Discipline someone.

Put in Work: Doing dangerous work for the set.

Put on Front Street: Snitched off.
Rat Packin': Many persons jumping on someone.
Ride: Car.
Ride On: Drive into enemy turf to start something.
Rock: Crack cocaine.
Rock Star: Cocaine prostitute.
Roller: Police radio car.
Rollin': Making a lot of money.
Ru: Piru gang member.
Saggin': Pants worn low off the hips.
Set: Gang.
Sherm/Wac-Wac: PCP.
Shot Caller: Gang leader.
Shot Out: Recognition.
Skeezer: Ugly girl.
Slangin': Selling dope.
Slippin': Careless, making mistakes.
Slob/Snoop: Crip name for blood.
Slow Your Roll: Slow down your life-style.
Smoked Out: Smoked all of your crack.
Smoker: Crack smoker.
Sprung: Crazy from smoking crack.
Stack It: Save.
Stay Out Of The Koolaid: Keep out of my business.
Strawberry: Girl who does sexual acts for drugs.
S'up?: What's up?
Take Out Of The Box: Murder someone.
Ten Rock: Ten-dollar piece of rock cocaine.
T.G.: Tiny gangster; youngster.
Throw Up Your Set (Let's See It, Put It In The Air Cuzz, Hit It Up Homes, Toss It Up): Flash your gang hand sign.
Toss Up: A girl who gives sex easily.
Trey-Eight: .38-caliber handgun.
Trippin': Doing crazy things.
Turkish Rope: Heavy gold necklace.
Tweakin': Needing more dope.
Twenty Rock: Twenty-dollar piece of rock cocaine.

What It "B" Like?: Blood greeting to homie.

What It "C" Like?: Crip greeting to homie.

What's Poppin'?: What's going on? What're ya doin'?

What's Shakin'?: Anything going on?

What Up?: Hello, hi. If said to an enemy gangster, a challenge.

What Up G?: Gangster greeting for another gangster.

4 ▶ People Nation and Folks Nation

CHICAGO HAS A LONG HISTORY OF ILLEGAL STREET GANGS THAT dates back more than 70 years. During the 1920s, the gangs formed inside the Illinois prisons and spread to the streets of Chicago when the inmates were paroled or their sentences expired. These early prison gangs were ruthless career criminals and, for the most part, Caucasian. Inside the prison walls they ran the prostitution, extortion, protection, gambling, loan sharking, and the contracting of hits. They threatened and intimidated other inmates and staff for canteen (food items, radios, cigarettes), money sent from home, drugs, sex, and other luxuries attainable in prison.

At the close of World War II, thousands of defense workers that had emigrated to Chicago to work in the defense factories were thrown out of work. A large proportion of them were black or Hispanic. Soon the prisons were filling up with these unemployed defense workers. During the 1950s and 1960s, the black and Hispanic inmates began organizing into tight-knit, powerful prison gangs. When the inmates were released, they continued with their gang affiliations and maintained contact with those still in prison. The result was a swelling of the ranks of the gangs both inside prison and on the streets. The largest gang to emerge from this beginning was the Blackstone Rangers, named after the intersection of 65th Street and Blackstone Avenue in Chicago.

During the 1980s, as the prison gang membership swelled, two factions within the walls emerged that fought for control of the illicit prison rackets. One of the groups was made up primarily of former members of the Blackstone Rangers, a group that professed to speak for and represent disadvantaged people. Its avowed intent was to build a nation for these people and call it the People Nation. The other group was the Disciples, whose avowed intent was to build a nation for all folks and call it the Folks Nation. This group could trace its lineage back to the 1960s, when they fought bloody engagements with the Blackstone Rangers on the streets of Chicago. Each faction developed its own rules, criminal intent, and distinct identifiers, and waged war inside the prison and outside on the Chicago streets. When a newcomer entered prison, especially if he had been part of a street gang, he hooked up with the group known to be supportive of his past affiliation, and he was given protection and the necessary commodities, making life within the walls somewhat bearable. Of course, by accepting this assistance, he became a debtor and would sooner or later be sent on a mission.

Soon nearly all of Chicago's illegal gangs, whether confined behind prison walls or racketeering on the city's south side, would claim either People or Folks. And they would wage a bloody war against each other, much the same as the Crips and Bloods were doing 2,000 miles away.

THE PEOPLE NATION

At their peak, the Blackstone Rangers boasted of a membership as high as 6,000. Their leader was an unschooled, Mississippi-born black man named Jeff Fort. The Blackstone Rangers carried on a bloody war with the Black Gangster Disciples until the mid-1960s, when Fort restructured the organization into 21 separate gangs, each with a titular head, forming a commission known as the Main 21. Fort named the new aggregation the Black P. Stone Nation. This renamed

Symbol of the People Nation. The 360-degree circle asserts that black
people once ruled the earth and will do so again. Fire represents the
suppression of the Black Nation (all black people worldwide) and their
inability to reach knowledge because of heat. Darkness is represented by
the shaded area above the hat, cane, and glove and refers to the black
majority of the world. The crescent moons represent the splitting of the
Black Nation into two parts, east and west. The five-point star represents
the eye of Allah watching over his people. The pyramid represents the
construction of the Egyptian pyramids by black people—not slaves, but
engineers and designers. It serves as a reminder of the mystery of how
the pyramids were constructed. The hat represents shelter, the cane
represents the staff of life, and the gloves represent purity.

structure immediately went after government money and came away with a federal grant to the tune of one million dollars from the Office of Economic Opportunity. This drew the ire of local politicians, who demanded an inquiry. In 1968 and 1969, the grant became the subject of a U.S. Senate investigation. During the investigation, Fort was brought before the committee and subsequently found guilty of contempt of congress and embezzlement of $7,500 in federal funds. He was sent to prison for five years.

Doing time, Fort began recruiting and forming a new gang, this one along Moorish religious lines. He called this new organization the El Rukns, which is the cornerstone of the Kaaba, a sacred shrine in Mecca, and ordained himself Prince Malik.

Whether sincere or not, operating under the guise of a Muslim religion, the El Rukns began to enjoy religious status. This opened up many doors within the prison that grant-

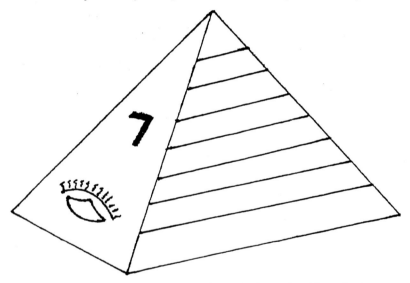

This pyramid is one of the symbols of the El Rukns, who ride under (are affiliated with) the People Nation. The eye signifies the all-seeing eye of Allah. The inverted L shows disrespect, possibly to the Latin Disciples.

ed special consideration to Fort and his followers. On the outside, his followers converted the Black P. Stone Nation headquarters at 3949 South Drexel into the El Rukns' Grand Major Temple.

In 1982, Fort returned to prison for 13 years after being found guilty of conspiracy to distribute cocaine. In 1987, Fort and four members of the El Rukns were found guilty of plotting terrorist acts on behalf of Libya's Colonel Muammar al-Qaddafi. Fort went to trial and received 80 years, but he continued to rule the El Rukns from within the prison walls.

Presidential hopeful Jesse Jackson, who has been rumored to be close to the El Rukns, publicly praised the organization for their assistance in a voter registration drive during his 1984 presidential campaign. The Chicago Police Department, however, labeled the El Rukns the ultimate street gang with a vast drug network that began with their own processing plant and distribution center and grossed hundreds of millions of dollars, which they in turn invested in legitimate businesses.

Aggressive police work started to take its toll on the El Rukns as myriads of the top echelon members and soldiers were hunted down and sent to prison. Alan Knox, an El Rukn general, admitted in federal court that he was responsible for six murders, including the deaths of two innocent bystanders and a killing in Greenville, South Carolina, by an El Rukn hit squad.

Today the El Rukns claim only a few hundred members and are not recruiting with vigor. They limit membership by invitation, open only to ex-convicts and family. This effectively screens out infiltrators. The leadership appears to be fairly stable. Internal strife is minimal.

Other gangs grew out of the El Rukns, such as the Black Stones, the Cobra Stones, the Egyptian Cobras, the Puerto Rican Cobras, and the Spanish Cobras. The El Rukns maintain strong contacts with these splinter groups and other People Nation gangs, such as the Vice Lords and the Latin Kings.

Latin Kings

The Latin Kings are a midwestern gang that rides under the People Nation. In a 1985 United States Department of Justice report entitled *Prison Gangs*, the Latin Kings were identified as the most violent of the Hispanic gangs: ". . . this group is the largest and most violent of the Latino gangs. They are affiliated with the Vice Lords." Other information revealed by this report is as follows.

Membership

Recruitment is open, but the gang attracts Latinos who are small in stature and violent. Members are either hardcore or of the aid-and-assist status. The gang patterns itself after Spanish royalty and features the crown (five- or three-point) with L on one side and K on the other. Black and gold are its colors.

Structure

Leadership is vaguely presented. If there is not one strong leader, the group uses a council with a titular head. The structure seems to be stable.

Organization and Operation of the Gang

Latin Kings tend to hold grudges and retaliate with violence. They project a macho image to obtain money and power. There is not much internal dissension.

Degree of Involvement in Criminal Activities

Latin Kings are frequently involved in assault, intimidation, and contraband weapons.

Two splinter groups of the Latin Kings, the Almighty Latin King Nation, a highly structured Puerto Rican and Hispanic gang, and the Almighty Latin King Charter Nation, are now fighting each other. Also, the Latin Kings are said to be recruiting actively in schools across the country.

The Latin Kings identify with the five-point crown, shown here. The upside-down pitchforks show disrespect to the Black Gangster Disciples and other Folks Nation gangs who use the pitchforks as one of their symbols.

Gangs Affiliated with the People Nation
Bishops
Black P. Stones
Cobra Stones
Cullerton Deuces
El Rukns
Gaylords
Insane Deuces

Insane Unknowns
Kents
Latin Counts
Latin Kings
Latin Saints
Mickey Cobras
Pachucos
Puerto Rican Stones
Spanish Lords
Vice Lords

Identification of People Nation Gang Members

Race

Blacks, Hispanics, and whites are accepted. The Latino gangs are made up primarily of Hispanics, although others are accepted if they meet the criteria. The other gangs are primarily black, with a small percentage of Hispanics and whites.

Symbols, Graffiti, Tattoos

The number 5, five-point star with crescent moon, five- or three-point crown, five dots, pyramid with crescent moon, top hat with cane and gloves, a pair of dice, a martini glass, playboy bunny, a dollar sign, and a walking cane are all symbols used by People Nation gang members in their graffiti, tattoos, and other identifiers.

Clothing

The dress code of People Nation gang members may be as casual as overalls and a shirt or as formal as a three-piece suit with a hat and tie. The real identifier is their insistence on shifting various articles of clothing toward the left side: an overall strap hanging down off the left shoulder, a cap tilted to the left, the left pant leg rolled up. Jogging shoes are worn with the left tongue up and the right tongue down and are often Converse gym shoes, since the logo is a five-point star.

The gangs affiliated with the People Nation identify with a five-point star, while the gangs affiliated with the Folks Nation identify with a six-point star. A slogan often used by the People Nation gang members is "Five alive, six must die." The six refers to all members of the Folks Nation.

Shoe laces may reflect gang colors. The left pant pocket may be turned out and exhibiting gang colors.

Hair

Their hair may be streaked on the left side or have designs cut into the left side: a five-point star, the number 5, a cane, crown, etc. Beads or barrettes of the gang's colors may also be worn.

Colors

Latin Kings and Vice Lords wear black and gold. Black P. Stone Nation and Mickey Cobras wear black, green, and red. El Rukns wear green and red.

Jewelry

Bracelets are worn on the left wrist. Belt buckles are worn on the left side. Rings, earrings, nose rings, stick-pins, all with gang symbols, are worn on the left side.

Hand Signs

Hand signs are always thrown up from the left side.

Hand sign for the Latin Kings.

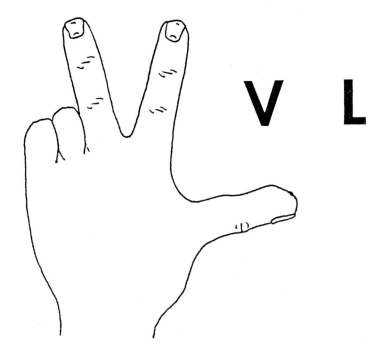

V L

The Vice Lords are affiliated with the Latin Kings. Their stronghold is in the larger cities in Illinois and adjacent states. There are about 20 factions of Vice Lords, the largest being the Conservative Vice Lords, followed by the Cicero Insane Vice Lords and the Unknown Vice Lords. This is their hand sign.

THE FOLKS NATION

The gangs that ride under the Folks Nation honor an affiliation with each other and consider all gangs under the People Nation to be enemies. Violent clashes occur when these two opposing factions meet. At stake is control of the lucrative street crime and prison rackets. They make amounts up to millions of dollars annually.

Black Gangster Disciple Nation

The largest midwestern gang to ride under the Folks Nation is the Black Gangster Disciple Nation (BGDN or BGDs). Recruitment is open. Most members are black; however, about 1 percent are white. The BGDs operate inside the midwestern prisons, as well as within the larger cities. Major activities are drug trafficking, weapons, gambling, protection, prostitution, and murder-for-hire.

The BGDs maintain a fairly stable structure. There is a recognized chain of command both within the prisons and on the outside. The leader is referred to as the King. Others of the hierarchy have titles as well. The gang is responsible for a large percentage of crime, and the King receives a cut of all profits. There have been episodes of internal dissension that have caused some of the members to break away and form their own splinter groups.

These splinter groups also ride under the Folks

The GD Prayer must be memorized by all gang members.

GD Prayer

 All GDs must use the knowledge on the six point star, 360 base on the life we belive and the love we have for one another. Wisdom is what we use to grow knowledge on the six point star in our nation flag in order to be real you must be willing to appear in front of Larry Hoover.

We believe in the teaching of our Honorable Chairman; in all laws and polices set forth by our Chairman and Executive Staff.

In the concept of ideology of the organization in aid and assisting our fellow brother of the struggle in all righteous Endeavors.

And standing strongly upon our six points utilizing Knowledge, Wisdom, and Understanding as we strive in our struggle for Education, Economical, and Political and Social Development that we are a special group of people with Integraty and Dignity.

In the vision of our great leader and through his vision we can be come a reckoning power of people beyond Boundaries without measures.

The GD Creed.

Nation and attempt to get along with the other Folks gangs. The Gangster Disciples (GDs) (sometimes known as the Disciple Nation), Black Disciples (BDs), and Black Gangsters (BGs), also known as the New Breed, are examples of gangs in this defection.

Some sources have indicated that the BGDs are attempting to unite all Disciple gangs. The BGDs have migrated westward and are now seen within the California and Nevada prison systems. Informed sources have said that Los Angeles now is home to about 1,000 of these transplants from the midwest. They are affiliated with the Brothers of the Struggle.

Brothers of the Struggle

During the summer of 1992, gang warfare erupted within Chicago's housing projects located along South Federal. Much blood was shed, including the massacre of children who had been caught in the crossfire. The police came down hard on the area and reported what most of the residents already knew, that the battles being waged were for control of the illicit drug trade within the projects by opposing gangs. And at the heart of the trouble was a relatively new Chicago gang that called itself Brothers of the Struggle—or BOS for short.

BOS rides under the Folks Nation, both in prison and on the outside. Documents recovered from the gang members were pieced together and assembled by investigating officers.

Note in this BOS Prayer the phrase "GDs and BDs has combined . . ." This indicates a unity of these three gangs: GDs, BDs, and BOS. Generally, all gangs that ride under the Folks Nation respect a mutual truce, although shaky at times, and consider all gangs under the People Nation their enemies.

BOS Prayer

*Looking out the window as
far as I can see,
All my BOS brothers standing
around me,
GD's and BD's has combined,
As we both unite our star will shine,
King David he recuted gave the (G)
Strength on the street,
He recuted the (D) on the history
of our G will last forever,
As the Brothers of the Struggle
Struggle together.*

Internal Rules of the B.O.S.

1. **SILENCE AND SECRECY.** No member should give any Information or discuss any matter that concerns any member or function of the organization to any individual that is not an outstanding member.
2. **DRUGS.** No member shall consume or inject any drugs that are addictive.
3. **STEALING.** No member shall steal from any convict inmate or resident.
4. **RESPECT.** No member shall be disrespectful to any member or non-member being disrespectful only intices other to become hotstely and be disrespectful to you which leads to unnecessary silly confrontation. always be respectful, dignified, honorable; loyal and thoughtful.
5. **BRAKEING AND ENTERING.** No member shall breake in or enter any building that cause un-due heat and presure tó other. Making institutional move that leads to lock-up and shake down is prohibited.
6. **GAMBLING.** No member shall gamble in any game unless all parties have there money up front.
7. **GUARD.** No member shell engage in any unnissery confrontation with any officers or administrative personnel.
8. **SPORTMANSHIP.** No member shell engage in heated arguments or fights while participating in any sports or games. Use good sportmenship at all time.
9. **PERSONAL-HYGENE.** All member must look presenable at all times and livin quarters should be kept clean.
0. **INCIDENTS.** All incidents minor or major concerning the health and well being of any member or members should be reported to the coordinators.
1. **AID AND ASSISTING.** All member shell Aid and assisting one another in all righteous endeavors.
2. **DUES.** All member are required to give 2 pack a month if able.

3. **EXERCISING.** All member are required to job three times around the yard and do fifty jumping jacks together at the beginning of each yard period except Saturday, Sunday and night yard.
4. **EXPLOITING.** No member shall use his membership, staff, or office to exploit or favor for any member.
5. **A.R. 504.** All member shall read and become familiar with the D.O.C. A.R. 504 administrative disaplene.
6. **RAPE.** No one should use threat or force to make anyone engage in any homosexual act.

Internal Rules
of the BOS.

DISCIPLINARY REPORT FORM USED BY THE B.O.S.

MINOR: _____
MAJOR: _____

TIME: _____
DATE: _____
INCIDENT: _____

WE BELIEVE IN THE TEACHING OF OUR HON-
ORABLE CHAIRMAN; IN ALL LAWS AND
POLICIES SET FORTH BY OUR CHAIRMAN
AND EXECUTIVE STAFF.

GD: ____

BD: ____   INCIDENT _____

NAME: ____   _____
                _____
                _____

IN THE CONCEPT OF IDEOLOGY OF THE ORGANIZATION
IN AID AND ASSISTING OUR FELLOW BROTHERS OF THE
STRUGGLE IN ALL RIGHTEOUS ENDEAVORS. IN THE
VISION OF OUR GREAT LEADER AND THROUGH HIS VI-
SION WE CAN BECOME A RECKONING POWER OF PEOPLE
BEYOND BOUNDARIES WITHOUT MEASURE.

WITNESS: _____
         _____
         _____

Disciplinary Report Form used by the BOS.

Another interesting piece of work is the Disciplinary
Report Form used by the BOS. The disciplinary form appears
to mimic that used by prison staff in disciplining inmates who
break prison rules. It is apparently used by the gang leaders
to discipline and track the gang members who violate their
own code of ethics, and not just within the prison. Many
Illinois gang investigators believe that the incarcerated BOS
leaders are also calling the shots from inside the prison system—issuing orders that must be carried out by the members on the streets.

Obviously, these documents contain many grammatical and spelling errors. However, the substance of the writings should be of interest to the attentive gang investigator.

Gangs Affiliated with the Folks Nation
Ambrose
Black Disciples
Black Gangster Disciple Nation
Black Gangster Disciples
C-Notes
Campbell Boys
Harrison Gents
Imperial Gangsters
Insane Popes
La Raza
Latin Disciples
Latin Dragons
Latin Eagles
Latin Jivers
Latin Lovers
Latin Souls
Orchestra Albany
Party People
Satan Disciples
Simon City Royals
Spanish Cobras
Spanish Gangsters: Two-Two Boys, Two-Sixers

Identification of Folks Nation Gang Members

Race
Blacks, Hispanics, and a sprinkling of whites are accepted. The Latino gangs are made up primarily of Hispanics. However, others are accepted if they meet the criteria.

Symbols, Graffiti, Tattoos
The number 6, the six-pointed star (Star of David), pitch-

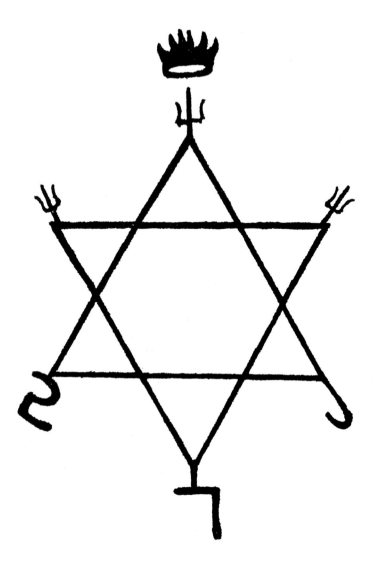

The six-pointed star, six-point crown riding atop the star, and upright pitchforks are all symbols of the Black Gangster Disciples, who ride under the Folks Nation. The upside-down number five, cane, and letter L are displayed as a sign of disrespect to the People Nation gangs that identify with these symbols.

forks, and a heart with flames or wings on both sides are used. A backward swastika is used by the Latin Disciples to honor their original leader, who was killed by the Latin Kings in 1970. His street name was Hitler. The backward swastika pays him honor without being mistaken for a white supremacist symbol.

Many black gangs like to use the playboy bunny as one of their emblems. A Playboy bunny with a cocked ear wearing a fedora and eyeglasses is used by the Two-Sixers, Black Gangster Disciples, King Hoovers (KHs), Simon City Royals (Folks), and KD (King David) Barksdales (David Barksdale was the founder of the BGDN and is now deceased). People Nation gangs, such as the Vice Lords, also use the Playboy bunny as one of their emblems, but usually, not always, both ears are straight up. To make a positive identification, the

The heart and wings are BGD symbols, as are the upright pitchforks. The number five and the cane are symbols of the People Nation. When displayed upside-down, as in this BGD tattoo, it shows disrespect toward any gang affiliated with the People Nation.

observer should look at the bunny's eyes, which may be five-point stars (for People Nation gangs) or six-point stars (for Folks Nation gangs).

When the enemy gang's graffiti is written upside down, it is a sign of disrespect and a challenge.

Clothing

Anything is acceptable, but an emphasis on the right side is obligatory: an overall strap hanging down off the right shoulder, a cap with the bill tilted toward the right, right shoe tongue up and left shoe tongue down, right pant leg rolled up, right pocket turned inside out, etc.

Hair

Their hair may be streaked on the right side. Designs such as the number 6, Star of David, BGD, or pitchforks may be cut into the right side. Beads or barrettes of the gang's colors may be worn.

Colors

Black Gangster Disciples, Black Disciples, and Latin Disciples wear black and blue. Two-Sixers wear tan and black.

Jewelry

Bracelets are worn on the right wrist. Belt buckles are worn on the right side. Rings, earrings, nose rings, stick-pins, all with gang symbols, are worn on the right side.

Hand Signs

Hand signs are always thrown up from the right side.

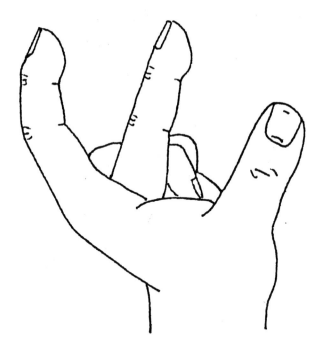

BGD

[PITCHFORK]

The pitchfork is simulated in this hand sign of the Black Gangster Disciples.

5 ▸ The Jamaican Posses

ORGANIZED CRIMINAL GROUPS HAVE HISTORICALLY DEMONSTRATED A propensity for violence. Few, however, have equaled the savagery attributed to the Jamaican Posses. (Note: When the word "posse" is capitalized it refers to members of the Jamaican Posses as opposed to its generic meaning when used in reference to other gangs in this book.) During home invasions, Posse members have tortured, mutilated, and killed all living beings in the house, including pregnant women, children, pets, and even goldfish.

Gunshots to the ankles, knees, and hips have been used as torture by Posse members attempting to elicit information from their victims before they kill them. Other forms of torture used by Posse members include hurling their victims into scalding baths. After the person dies, the body is dismembered and the gory parts are scattered around the countryside. This is known as "jointing."

Posse members suspected of informing, pilfering, or in any way interfering with the goals of the group are summarily executed as quickly as are Posse enemies. Witnesses have been interviewed by the police—and revealed nothing—only to be put to death as a warning to others not to talk to police. In February 1988, Posse members gunned down four of their own people—Jamaican women, one of whom was four weeks pregnant—in Washington, D.C. Responding police, who had to break into the house, found four children, ages 16 months to three years, crying over the bloody bodies.

On December 7, 1987, a commercial plane carrying 43 persons crashed in the mountains north of San Luis Obispo, California, killing all aboard. Investigators determined that a passenger, David Burke, a Jamaican, had smuggled a .44 Magnum pistol onto the plane and, after the plane was in flight, shot and killed his former boss, who was also on the plane. He then turned the gun on the pilot and the copilot, causing the plane to plunge to the earth.

For decades, Jamaicans have grown, harvested, and smuggled high grade marijuana into the United States. During the early 1980s, the Jamaican Posse members entering the United States dealt mainly in the distribution of marijuana. As they began to prosper, more nationals entered the United States, and they began to traffic in cocaine and crack cocaine. Inevitably, they moved in against other established drug traffickers including the Cubans and Colombians. Wars for control of drug territories ensued, and by January 1985, the BATF (Bureau of Alcohol, Tobacco, and Firearms) had launched a national investigation aimed against Jamaican organized crime for weapons trafficking. Shipment routes were long established, the main point of entry into the United States being the southern tip of Florida, with secondary sites located in Texas. The Jamaicans were thought to have been responsible for over 1,000 homicides nationwide.

Law enforcement officers caught up in the web of Jamaican organized crime have been targeted by the Jamaican Posses. Police in Virginia reported that a contract of $25,000 had been put out by the Jamaicans for anybody who killed a policeman. The Jamaicans utilize countersurveillance tactics in an ongoing effort to identify and eliminate law enforcement officers who are investigating them. They seek to learn the home addresses of police and federal agents, as well as their telephone and beeper numbers.

In addition to high-powered weapons, Posse members have also been arrested for carrying explosives, including grenades and homemade bombs. In March 1988, a member of the Shower Posse was arrested in Hartford, Connecticut. Inside his residence, police found narcotics as well as a hand grenade and soldier-of-fortune type manuals detailing the manufacture of plastic explosives.

On December 17, 1987, a New York police officer and two civilians were gunned down during a Brooklyn gunfight. Guns used in the battle were traced to the Delroy Edwards organization in New York City. The Edwards organization was confirmed to be an arm of Jamaican organized crime that included two Jamaican Posses—the Rankers and the Southie Posses.

Delroy Edwards and four of his henchmen were arrested on March 11, 1988. Edwards was linked to six homicides and thought to have been involved in a dozen others. The high-ranking Posse members arrested along with him were charged with federal crimes, including drug trafficking, weapons violations, assault, and immigration violations. Authorities estimated the organization was bringing in up to $100,000 daily.

Forty Posses have now been identified that operate coast to coast in the United States. These can all be traced to specific neighborhoods in Jamaica, where they originally developed along geographical lines much the same way as the Hispanic barrios. With the arrival of crack cocaine in this country, the Jamaican Posse members entered the United States in droves, mainly as illegal aliens. These Posses differ from other organized drug traffickers in that they act as importers, wholesalers, and distributors, which returns to them a much higher margin of profit than the traffickers who use middlemen (Cubans and Colombians usually limit their operation to the wholesale market). At the street level, a Posse that can manage 50 crack houses can realize a profit of $9 million a month.

Some of the seediest areas in some of the largest U.S. cities are controlled exclusively by Jamaican Posses. Any outsider coming into the area to sell drugs walks a thin line between life and death. Those that are allowed to sell drugs must pay a "tax" to the ruling Posse. A CBS television report ("West 57th Street," March 19, 1988) revealed that Posse drug profits paid for high-powered weaponry that was shipped back to Jamaica in support of island politics that traditionally have been marked by violence. Many of the Posse criminals operating in the United States and politicians back on the island profess to be Rastafarians.

RASTAFARIANS

Haile Selassie, the last emperor of Ethiopia, died in Addis Ababa in 1975. His true name was Lij Tafari Makonnen. When he was only 16 years old, he was appointed governor of Sidamo Province and became Ras (Duke) Tafari. Tafari weathered many crises both from within and without, including the invasion of Ethiopia by Mussolini in 1935.

Tafari concentrated heavily on foreign affairs and, as regent in 1923, was able to get Ethiopia admitted into the League of Nations. In 1928, he was granted the title of negus (King). Acutely aware of the plight of the black Africans living in foreign countries, Salassie decreed that all should eventually migrate back to Africa, specifically Ethiopia. As the years passed, he began to amass a large following and soon declared himself to be the living God.

On the island of Jamaica, where 90 percent of the population are descendants of slaves, Selassie gathered many adherents. This trend continues to this day. Many Rastafarians are associated with Jamaican organized crime; many others are not.

The Doctrine

The brethren are endowed with the doctrine at birth. As they mature and willingly accept his Eminence, Ras Tafarian, as God, they will make secret vows agreeing to conform to the ideals of the movement and undergo secret initiation rites. Among their beliefs are:

• Ras Tafari is the living God.

- Ethiopia is the black man's home.
- Repatriation is the way of redemption for black men.
- The ways of the white man are evil.
- Eating pork is forbidden.
- The herb, marijuana or ganja, is a gift of God, who enjoined us to smoke it.
- Beards and long hair are enjoined on men; it is a sin to shave or cut the hair. Dreadlocks are characteristic of the preferred hair style.
- Alcohol use and gambling are forbidden.

JAMAICAN POSSES IN THE UNITED STATES

Forty Jamaican Posse gangs operating in many of the largest U.S. cities have been identified by law enforcement agencies. There are probably more. They are involved in violent crime including murders, drug trafficking, robberies, kidnappings, home invasions, money laundering, and gang warfare. There are in excess of 10,000 Posse members spread throughout the 40 known Posses, which are:

Back Bush Posse
Banton Posse
B & E Posse
Bilbour Posse
Bushmouth Posse
Cuban Posse
Dog Posse
Dreadnox
Dunkirk Posse
Exodus Posse
Flethees Land Posse
Forties Posse
Jungle Posse
Jungle Lites Posse
Lockie Daley Organization
Markham Massive

Marvally Posse
Montego Bay Posse
Nanyville Posse
Nineties Posse
Okra Slime Posse
Paneland Posse
Public Enemy Number One
Reema Posse
Renkers Posse
Riverton City Posse
Rude Boys
Samocan Posse
Shower Posse
Southie Posse
Spangler Posse
Spanish Town Posse
Stiker Posse
Super Posse
Superstar Posse
Tel Aviv Posse
Tivoli Gardens Posse
Towerhill Posse
Trinidadian Posse
Waterhouse Posse

The Junglelites

The Jungle is a township in Jamaica. Many of the inhabitants are violent criminals and are called Junglelites. They have left such a trail of violence that their name has become synonymous with "murderers."

There is a Posse called the Jungle Lite Posse and one called Jungle Posse. These two Posses can trace their lineage back to the Jungle, and they also have connections to Jamaican organized crime.

The Posses, in a way, are structured like a football team. Their name may be taken from a specific area, but their members may not all be from that same area. They could have found their way to specific Posses by avenues other than the same township in Jamaica. For instance, the Jungle Posse has been identified in Kansas City, Miami, New York, and Philadelphia. This Posse could have picked up recruits or replacements from any of these areas, the only requirement being that they are Jamaican.

IDENTIFICATION OF JAMAICAN POSSES

The following are some common characteristics of Jamaican Posse gang members.

- Posse gangsters prefer high-powered weapons; they shun Saturday Night Specials and other small handguns.
- They make use of sophisticated countersurveillance tactics.
- They may resist arrest and be quick to use their weapons.
- They use fake names, IDs, and forged immigration documents.
- The Jamaicans and Rastafarians speak an English that may be hard to understand by our standards; it has a distinct Calypso or island dialect.
- Their language reflects their religious beliefs and the unity they feel. In their speech, they use "I words" to express this unity. For example, the plural of I to them is "I and I," not us or we. This is also seen as "I-n-I." Myself becomes "I-self," and ourselves becomes "I-n-I self." When a group of them are engaged in conversation, it becomes very difficult for law enforcement personnel to understand what they are saying.

JAMAICAN GANG TERMINOLOGY

Babylon: The Establishment; the government.
Baldhead: Undesirable, not a Rasta.
Battyman: Gay.
Beast: Police.
Binghi: Brother; affectionate term for a friend.

Bite: Arrest.
Blood Clot: Bad.
Brigade: Junglelite; murderer.
Brother: Fellow Jamaican.
Bucky: Shotgun.
Bumbaclot: Motherfucker.
Check It Out: Evaluate a potential robbery or other crime.
Check You Out: Come to visit.
Chombo: Derogatory term for a West Indian.
Clap: Shoot.
Crown: Hat; tam.
Dawta: Woman.
Dread: The state of fearlessness in the face of all obstacles that a person possesses; a serious situation.
Dreadlocks: Braided Rasta hair style.
Dunzi: Money.
Front-Liners: Junglelites; murderers.
Ganja (Corn, Food, Ily, Herb): Marijuana.
Gate: House, apartment.
Gong (Puppy, Tool, Dog): Gun.
Gun Dog: Gun, weapon; gunman.
Hot Steppers: Pickpocket; wanted gang member.
I-n-I: Me; me and God.
I-n-I Self: Ourselves.
Ily: Sensamilla.
Iney: "Everything is great"; a greeting.
Iree: Most righteous.
Iree-Ites: Higher than the most righteous.
Irle/Iry/Irey: A greeting; goodness; a state often arrived at through smoking weed or reasoning.
I-Self: Myself.
Jah: God.
Juke: Holdup.
Junglelite: Murderer; resident of the Jamaican township called the Jungle.
Likk: Shoot.
Machine: Machine gun.

Manifest: Plan a crime.
Mash It Up: You handle it.
Mon: Man.
Pussyclot: Unpleasant.
Ras: From Amarhic meaning head, chief, or king; a title a Rastafarian uses before his name.
Ras Clot: Worse than a blood clot.
Ras Tafari: Haile Selassie, the Lion of Judah, head of the Rastafarians.
Rasta: Name by which the Jamaicans call the Ras Tafari.
Rings: Guns and bullets.
Roots: Reggae music, the most spiritual.
Rudeboys: Young Rastas.
Seen: Used instead of "yes"; used to clarify if a person is in agreement and understands all realities being reasoned upon.
Shit, Stem: Society, the system.
Shooty: Shotgun.
Spliff (pronounced spleef): Joint. Four spliffs are equal to 1 ounce.
Steep: Hot, wanted by the police; hard times.
Step: To move; leave; get away from trouble.
Teeth: Bullets.
Trans: Car.
Yard: Jamaica, West Indies.
Yasty, Yus: Clothes.
Yellow Paper: Phony Canadian 50-dollar bill.
York: New York.
You No See: You fail to understand.

Asian/South Sea Islander Gangs

FOLLOWING THE END OF THE VIETNAM WAR IN 1975, SAIGON was taken over and occupied by communist forces. A mass exodus of refugees fled South Vietnam seeking asylum in other countries, mainly the United States. Makeshift boats carried tens of thousands of these refugees away from their homeland. Thousands of them perished in the attempt, but thousands more reached foreign shores. Other Southeast Asians seeking a better life elsewhere began fleeing their homelands as well. Authorities in California estimate upwards of 500,000 of these refugees found their way to the Golden State.

The majority of newly arrived aliens were Vietnamese. Others were Chinese/Vietnamese, Laotians, and Cambodians. The Chinese/Vietnamese assimilated into the Chinese-American communities. The other groups moved toward communities where people of their own ethnic backgrounds had settled. Most of these arrivals had a strong family discipline, were hard working and law abiding, and had a strong desire to succeed. Others did not.

Many of the recent arrivals came from shattered families, were battle worn, bitter, and cared little for human life or property. Some of the Vietnamese/Chinese youths, known as Viet Chings, found instant employment as runners, enforcers, drug and weapons couriers, and gunmen for Chinese organized crime. The Chinese triads recruited heavily from this newly arrived labor pool.

The Vietnamese who moved toward a criminal life-style excelled in home invasions, protection, torture, murder-for-hire, and extortion of small family run restaurants and other businesses. They became experts at car theft and chop shop operations and usually stayed within the confines of their own ethnic communities when committing criminal acts. They knew their victims would not go to the police. The law-abiding newcomers—the victims—had grown up in Southeast Asia under the thumb of a corrupt government and police system and distrusted police and other uniformed personnel. This made it easy for those committing the crimes.

The Vietnamese gangsters soon began moving to other U.S. cities to engage in robberies, burglaries, and home invasions, always staying within the Asian communities. They soon set a pattern of committing a crime of violence in a city with a large Asian community, then quickly moving on to another city. Soon these traveling gangsters had fixed routes crisscrossing the United States. One day, they could pull a home invasion in Sacramento, and the next day, a robbery in Portland. They became known as Vietnamese traveling gangs and preferred Japanese cars, multiseat vans, and air transportation. The criminal elements of the Cambodian and Laotian immigrants followed the same pattern as their Vietnamese brothers and sisters. The females were there to conceal the weapons if stopped by the police, to distract the police, to gain entrance into the homes targeted for invasion, and to provide comfort to the men.

The Asian youth gangs we see today are the offspring of these refugees from the Vietnam War. They have formed their own street gangs, much like the blacks and Hispanics. They have taken names such as the Oriental Boyz (OB), Sacramento Nip Boys (SNB), Oriental Killer Boys (OKB), Born To Kill (BTK), Tiny Rascal Gang (TRG), Masters of Destruction (MOD), and many others. These Asian Americans, along with South Sea Islanders such as the Tongan Crip Gang (TCG), Samoan

Warriors (SW), and Philippine gangs such as the Bahala Na, stockpile weapons, war against each other, and act much like our homegrown gangs. Like their older role models, they, too, excel in auto theft, drug trafficking, and weapons. A favorite method used by many Asian gangs to obtain weapons is the smash-and-grab break-in. A car or van (usually stolen) driven by gang members accelerates and crashes into a storefront, most often a gun store or a pawn shop. This sets off an alarm, and the gangsters have only a matter of seconds to clean out all the store's guns (handguns preferred) and get away before the police arrive. Accomplices waiting in another vehicle quickly load the weapons, the gangsters pile in, and the getaway vehicle roars away. Sometimes a chase car—a beat up car of little value driven by a gang member whose job it is to crash into the police vehicle, if necessary, to facilitate a getaway—is also put to use.

ILLEGAL TRAFFICKING IN THE COMPUTER INDUSTRY

Other Indo-Chinese and Vietnamese gang activity centers around stolen computer chips. In California's Silicon Valley, microprocessors about the size of a poker chip and worth more than any drug or precious metal are being stolen and sold through organized Asian gangs. Companies making these computer brains have lost tens of millions of dollars worth of these untraceable chips. The San Jose Police Department has a high-tech task force assigned to the investigation of computer chip crime and the apprehension of those responsible. Their investigators have stated that the computer chips are worth their weight in gold, ". . . and there's an organized network out there to buy them even if they're stolen. There's a constant market for the stuff." In Westminster, California, fences repackage and distribute the chips throughout the United States and overseas, particularly in Asian countries. "The Asian gangs seem to be controlling this down here," said Westminister Police Detective Marcus Frank, and he added, "The amount of traffic [in hot computer chips] has got to rival the narcotics trade. This has all the elements of drug crimes too, with hand-to-hand buys, couriers carrying the stuff, reverse stings."

VIETNAMESE TRAVELING GANGS

For several years, Vietnamese traveling gangs have terrorized other Asians who are trying to assimilate into the American mainstream through hard work and family-run businesses. These Vietnamese mobile criminals continue to crisscross the United States, preying on the local Vietnamese communities. In home invasions, the gangs crash through the front door of Asian homes waving guns, robbing, torturing, and raping the occupants in a savage reign of terror. When finished, the gang members roar off, many times in stolen cars, only to reappear in a distant city days later. The hapless victims, who had learned to distrust and fear the police back in their homeland, rarely complain to the local authorities. This perpetuates the problem, as other gangsters within their own communities often shake them down for protection after the rampage.

Other crimes often attributed to the roving Vietnamese are auto theft (they prefer late model Toyotas and Hondas) and credit card fraud. In Reno, September 1992, four Vietnamese nationals were arrested after the Cal Neva casino complained to authorities that they had defrauded the casino out of thousands of dollars by using phony credit cards. The four, identified as Canadian citizens, were thought to be members of a notorious Asian gang, the Big Circle Boys (BCB). Canadian authorities allege the gang is responsible for most of the $50 million in credit card fraud in that country this past year.

The four Vietnamese arrested in Reno were tried and convicted in Reno District Court for using a forged credit card. The sentence was handed down by Judge Mills Lane the day before Christmas. Judge Lane failed to establish a direct connection between the four and the BCB. He then stated he wanted to send a message "all the way to Canada" and formally sentenced the four nationals to two years in prison. Unfortunately, given the relatively light sentence, this may have been the wrong message to send.

In testimony before the U.S. Senate subcommittee on investigations in June 1992, the BCB was identified as having its roots in Hong Kong and China, with branches extending into North America and Canada. Credit card fraud was only one of the gang's illegal enterprises. According to testimony, the gang was responsible for the importation of 800 to 1,200 pounds of heroin into the United States between 1988 and 1990. Estimated profits were calculated to be $72 million.

Among other criminal enterprises, the gang is known to be in the business of smuggling illegal aliens into the United States and Canada. During the past two years, the gang is thought to have smuggled in as many as 1,200 illegals at an average cost of $20,000 per person. They are being assisted in their endeavors by the Fuk Ching or Fukienese Youth Gang of New York, which is reportedly one of the most violent street gangs in New York City.

American law enforcement officials believe the BCB is led by a naturalized American citizen—a Vietnamese-born woman. Many of the gang members are former Chinese soldiers or ex-Red Guards, the shock troops of the late Mao Tse-Tung. These criminals are said to be skilled in hand-to-hand combat and military weaponry. Although immigration laws have been tightened in recent years, in the past when they were arrested here and in Canada, they often did not fear deportation since it was fairly easy for them to claim refugee status and be granted asylum.

LAOTIAN GANGS

In May 1992, Las Vegas District Judge Joseph Pavlikowski handed down a 50-year prison sentence to Somsanak "Soviet" Maokhamphiou after finding him guilty of a smash-and-grab break-in of a Nellis Boulevard gun store.

Maokhamphiou, a Laos native, was identified as the leader of an Asian gang with roots in Southern California. The gang specialized in crashing into storefronts late at night, usually in stolen trucks or cars, and then stripping the store of guns and ammunition. The most sought-after weapons were easily concealable handguns.

It was brought out during the trial that Maokhamphiou had a criminal history that included 43 arrests and time served in California prisons. Few felt that he deserved less than the 50 years except his attorney, who argued that his client was given more time than most killers.

Had the sentence stood up, Maokhamphiou would not have been eligible for parole until he had served 12 years flat. However, during the Post Conviction Relief hearing, his 50-year sentence was whittled down to only 10 years, making him parole eligible after serving only one-third of the 10-year revised sentence.

The guns taken by Maokhamphiou and his mob were to be used in extortion attempts targeted toward other Asians—including Asian gangs as well as Asian businesses. In Sacramento, there are upwards of a dozen Laotian gangs, many at war against each other. For example, the Sacramento Bad Boys in Oak Park are at war with the Polk Street Boys. The Bad Boys claim Blood. (This does not mean they are aligned with the Bloods from Los Angeles, only that they are trying to add to their reputation for ruthlessness.) The 916 Laos, Polk Street Boys, Dragon Boys, and STC Laos claim Crip (for the same reasons). Gang warfare has erupted between the Sacramento Bad Boys, who are backed up by the 916 Laos and Dragon Boys, and the Polk Street Boys.

Traditionally, Asian gangsters have victimized only others of their own race. There is mounting evidence that this is changing. The Laotians that have immigrated into this country may be the first Asian ethnic group to break out of this stereotype. The Laotian nationals, having a reputation as the most violent of the Asians, are now staking out turf in the cities where they have settled. Recent shootings in Sacramento involving Laotian suspects have been against black and Hispanic gang members.

CAMBODIANS

In Long Beach's Little Phnom Penh section, Cambodian refugees trying to realize the American dream find themselves locked into a different kind of war. Hispanic gang bangers from the East Side Longos barrio have fired into their homes during drive-by shootings attempting to harass and intimidate. The Cambodians, long accustomed to hardship and blood, have in turn formed their own gangs to repel the domestic enemy.

In October 1989, Cambodian gangsters killed their first East Side Longo in a retaliatory drive-by. The Hispanics were quick to learn that many of these newly arrived Asians had been hardened to violence in their homeland, where suffering and hardship were part of growing up, and they were not likely to turn the other cheek. The Cambodians formed several gangs, including the Long Beach Asian Boyz, the Tiny Rascals, the Crazy Brozers Clan, and the Korat Boyz. As of this writing, the Cambodians and the East Side Longos continue to fight.

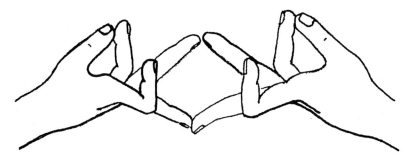

c/o Schober

korat boyz

Hand sign for the Korat Boyz.

CHINESE TRIADS

Chinese triad societies trace their beginning to the seventeenth century. Initially, one of their prime objectives was to rid China of all foreigners. What has evolved from this seems to be nothing more today than organized crime, Chinese style. The triads are rigidly structured and operate solely for the conquest of money. Strict adherence to the code of silence and secrecy is followed by all. The use of fear, intimidation, and the threat of death are used worldwide by the triads to ensure nothing stands in the way of their success. These Chinese criminal organizations have five major characteristics:

- Recognized leadership
- Sharply defined territory
- Strict code of discipline
- Emphasis on silence
- Organization

The term "triad" itself is not a Chinese term but rather an English term used to describe the organization's symbol. This symbol is a triangle with the sides representing the three powers of heaven, earth, and man.

Also, the term should not be confused with the Chinese tongs, which in America were an outgrowth of the Chinese laborers' existence during the development of the early West: Laundry Tongs, Medicine Tongs, Railroad Tongs, etc. Back then, Chinese immigrants could join the local tongs and find com-

Chinese triad symbol. The three sides represent heaven, earth, and man.

panionship, assistance, and guidance. (Although now, many tongs commonly have connections to Asian organized crime.)

In China, the BCB gang has formed alliances with the 14K Triad to operate prostitution and karaoke bars in the southern provincial capital of Canton. "Big Circle" is Chinese slang for Canton. Regardless of where they operate—whether in China or worldwide—they, like all other Chinese triads, maintain close ties with Hong Kong. Organized street gangs like the Ghost Shadows and the Flying Dragons that are known to exist in every Chinese community in the United States and Canada also maintain close ties with the Hong Kong criminal hierarchy.

Informed sources indicate there may be as many as 80,000 hard-core triad members based in Hong Kong. This forms the nucleus of a worldwide criminal enterprise that brings in billions of dollars annually through extortion, prostitution, money laundering, gambling, and illegal drugs. These secret societies also control the world's supply of heroin. During the frequent meetings held in Hong Kong, countries from the four corners of the earth send emissaries into the colony. Of major importance to the triads is the imminent takeover of Hong Kong by the mainland Chinese in 1997. Many are in the process of moving their empires out of the colony into the Asian centers in Europe, Canada, and the United States. San Francisco has been selected to be the first U.S. city to absorb this influx.

Initiates entering one of the triads are thoroughly screened before being granted admittance. Their backgrounds are checked carefully, and they must have family or close acquaintances already within the organization. And of course, they must be Chinese. This virtually precludes the planting of infiltrators by the police. By the time he passes through the initiation rites (which include drinking wine containing the blood of all those present), the recruit's entire life will have been placed under a microscope.

Wo Hop To Triad

Peter Chong, alleged head of the Wo Hop To Triad (WHT) in San Francisco, has received hundreds of thousands of dollars over the past few years from Chan Tinghung, identified by a senate investigation committee as the head of the Wo Hop To Triad in Hong Kong.

The Wo Hop To (Harmonious Union Plan) is the first Chinese triad to have been transplanted from Asia to the United States. The WHT was founded in 1908 in Sai Ying Pun, western Hong Kong, and is thought to have roots in ancient secret societies. The triad was politically oriented, aligning itself with the Republican government in China to fight against the Imperial Ching government. They first solicited donations from local businesses and eventually moved into organized crime, including prostitution, narcotics, trafficking, and extortion.

With the impending takeover of Hong Kong by mainland China on the horizon, the triad focused on San Francisco as its first U.S. target. The WHT leaders carefully outlined their strategy. The ruling Chinatown gang in San Francisco at the time was the Wah Ching. The WHT had decided to use persuasion in their dealings with the Wah Ching, but the objective of the WHT was to gain absolute control of the criminal enterprises in San Francisco's Chinatown, and if the Wah Ching resisted, the WHT would take over by brute force.

The Wah Ching weren't about to give up the lucrative Chinatown rackets to the Wo Hop To. Consequently, both sides prepared for war. Hundreds of guns were bought illegally. The Wo Hop To also ordered 300 bulletproof vests. Shooters were recruited by both sides, and the war began in earnest.

In April 1990, Wah Ching member Danny Vuong, 23, was shot and killed outside of Cat's Nightclub. In May 1990, Wo Hop To member Michael Bit Chen Wu, 37, was shot to death outside the Purple Onion Nightclub. Several alleged Wo Hop To leaders were wounded, including Tony Poon, 47, who is the brother-in-law of San Francisco police commissioner Pius Lee. In March 1991, Hung Quoc Duong, a leader of the

Vietnamese Red Fire gang who had joined the Wo Hop To, was garroted in the Oakland hills.

When the violence finally subsided, the Wo Hop To was the new ruling Chinatown gang. They had successfully muscled out the Wah Ching and seized control of loan sharking, credit card fraud, gambling, extortion, and narcotics trafficking.

The Wo Hop To, now firmly established in the land of opportunity, set their sights on the biggest prize of all: a worldwide scheme to supplant cocaine with heroin—the drug the Asians controlled—and attain the extraordinary profits.

BETTER LIVING THROUGH CHEMISTRY

The chain of events begins in the mountains of Southeast Asia in an area covering more than 150,000 square miles. This region extends across parts of Laos, Thailand, and northeastern Burma as well as parts of China, and is known as the Golden Triangle. For thousands of years, the Golden Triangle has given life to the opium poppy, and in so doing, has brought about gratifying relief from pain, sought-after euphoria, and untold misery to millions of the earth's inhabitants.

Every year in late August or early September, an army of peasant farmers scatter tons of poppy seeds in fields throughout the Golden Triangle. These tiny seeds are carefully nurtured for about three months. As the plants near maturity, the stems reach a height of about four feet and support a single pea pod embraced by large, colorful petals. As the blossoms continue to age, the petals begin to drop. The seedpods, about the size of a small egg, are tapped by the peasants, and a milky-white fluid oozes out and gathers on the surface. Overnight the sap begins to set, yielding a blob no bigger than a pea that takes on a dark brown appearance—the sought-after raw opium.

The peasant workers collect the opium, and, when their work is completed, the hill tribes throughout the Golden Triangle will have removed from the region well over 1,500 tons of raw opium. These hill tribes will accept something close to $40 per kilo of raw opium, which represents the approximate yield of one-half acre. After this kilo has been refined and stepped on repeatedly, it will be packaged into thousands of bindles and will bring in excess of $200,000 when delivered and sold to the addicts of the world.

In the jungle laboratories, skilled chemists convert the raw opium into morphine. Some of the morphine will be converted to heroin in the same jungle labs; much more will be shipped to other, more sophisticated laboratories in Hong Kong and elsewhere, where highly skilled and highly paid Chinese chemists will extract nearly pure heroin from the morphine.

Two kinds of heroin can be produced at this stage. One has a purity of approximately 70 percent and may only be used for smoking since it will clog a syringe. The heroin at this stage is referred to as heroin number three. To produce injectable heroin, heroin number four, further refining is necessary. The resulting product, which will eventually be distributed to addicts worldwide, is nearly 99 percent pure and known around the world as China White.

As the China White begins its worldwide passage, it will be reduced in purity—stepped on—at each stop. Cornstarch, lactose, flour, and quinine are some of the more preferred substances used to cut heroin. When the product has arrived at its final destination (the street-level addict), the heroin will have been reduced to something like 3 percent purity. Despite the reduced purity, the addict injecting this product will still realize an effect nearly three times that of medical morphine. And his addiction will cost hundreds or even thousands of dollars a week.

For the heroin addict who has fallen so far that he can no longer steal enough to support the endless craving for China White, he may have to settle for another form of heroin—a product abundant with contaminants. This product is not of Asia, but of Mexico, and it is so alarmingly addictive, it may replace crack cocaine as the number one illegal street drug in the industrialized countries of the world—black tar heroin.

The Black Dragon

Black tar heroin, a product of Mexico, has its start in the poppy fields of Sinaloa, Durango, and Chihuahua. Most of these fields are much smaller and harder to detect than those in the Golden Triangle, but the process of cultivation is much the same.

When the raw opium is bled from the plant and collected by the Mexican *campesinos* (peasants), *acaparadores*—gatherers—buy the raw opium and move it to clandestine mobile laboratories that operate throughout the Sierra Madre region where it will be converted into black tar. At this stage of production, the *campesino* will receive approximately $600 per kilogram of raw opium.

Black tar heroin, which can be processed in as little as one to three days, may be moist and sticky like roofing tar or as hard and black as coal. It will be known as junk, tootsie roll, or goma. Whatever its name or consistency, it will be identifiable by its nauseating vinegarlike stench. Chemicals used in the manufacturing process are substituted freely and measurements are not exact. Short cuts are often employed. As a result, the product contains many contaminants, and the purity varies. Depending on the particular batch, the end product that reaches the street-level addict may vary by as much as 40 percent in purity. Even after being stepped on, black tar may have a purity level of anywhere between 40 and 80 percent. The addict can never be sure of the potency of the product, which is one reason there are so many deaths from black tar. (A few years ago, in Unit 7, a maximum-security lockup unit at Nevada State Prison, two inmates overdosed on black tar. One was revived and the other died.)

The number one market for Mexican black tar is—no surprise—the United States. Getting the tar to market is relatively easy. Migrant farm workers and illegal aliens often pay their way into the United States by smuggling black tar. Other Mexicans take advantage of the lightly guarded 2,000-mile border separating the two countries and make nightly forays into this country under cover of darkness. Other runners cross the border at customs stations carrying the product concealed in baby diapers, stashed within body cavities, or hidden inside battered cars and pickups.

Once the drug has been smuggled in, it is quickly moved up to the next link in the chain: barrios within the Hispanic community. There it will be stepped on, packaged, and moved farther on up the line. Prior to being stepped on, the black tar will have a purity level of somewhere between 65 and 85 percent. Random samples sometimes test out at more than 90 percent purity.

Black tar heroin is cut with sugar or over-the-counter medications, such as diphenhydramine (an antihistamine) or Dormin (a sleeper). Diphenhydramine, used in cold remedies, helps to alleviate the side effects of tar usage, such as a runny nose and sleepiness. Frequently, a blender is used to mix the tar and cutting agent. Addicts at times merely roll softened tar and sugar together in waxed paper.

The large-scale distributors of black tar heroin will package the product into pieces—Mexican ounces—and by the time it reaches the street addict, it will cost in the neighborhood of $150 to $500 a gram. The kilogram of black tar that the *campesino* sold for $600, after processing and being made ready for sale in the United States, will bring in about $150,000.

The effect of heroin on the person is directly opposite that of cocaine. Though both drugs are highly addictive, cocaine excites and stimulates the central nervous system, making it an ideal party drug—a groupie drug. Heroin, on the other hand, has the opposite effect. It calms while rewarding the user with a feeling of great exhilaration, a euphoria that the individual appreciates within himself. Of course, as with all illegal hard drugs, when the effects wear off, deep depression and paranoia often follow.

HEROIN COMES TO THE UNITED STATES

"If God made anything better than heroin, he kept it for himself." The man who made this flat statement was a 46-

year-old Vietnam veteran recounting his wartime experience. "Frank" was a clean-shaven prison inmate serving multiple sentences for a series of armed robberies. Frank, along with 100,000 other servicemen returning from the Vietnam War, brought his heroin addiction with him.

In Nam, teenage working girls enticed GIs into bed with a promise of night-long recreation of sex and drugs. After weeks or months on the line, few Americans resisted. Marijuana was okay, but heroin number three, cheap and plentiful, was both potent and smokable—and highly addictive.

The U.S. government's involvement in Southeast Asia was bringing undreamed of prosperity and corruption to the area, and in so doing, was transforming the Golden Triangle from a minor opium producing region into a multibillion-dollar yearly enterprise responsible for 70 percent of the world's opium supply. The Hong Kong-based Chinese triads were monitoring the area closely. Advanced guards of the Wo Shing Wo Triad were sent to Saigon along with scouts from the 14K Triad to evaluate the situation. The reports sent back to Hong Kong were encouraging: the Americans could easily be hooked, and, once hooked, they were willing to pay whatever the traffic would bear.

With the pullout of U.S. troops from the region in the 1970s, the supply far exceeded the demand. Not that the Asian inhabitants were any less addicted than the Americans, but during the U.S. military involvement, it is estimated that the opium warlords had been processing more than 20 tons of the drug a year. The Chinese triads that had been investing heavily in the venture were now determined not only to maintain their drug empire, but to expand it worldwide.

The next few years brought a wave of Chinese organized crime figures to secret meetings in Hong Kong. The meetings were attended by the elite of higher echelon Asian criminals. Many could trace their criminal lineage back for generations. Nearly all continents were represented. Strategies were discussed, planned, and voted on.

The triads had the product, China White. But they also

acknowledged that their competition, the cocaine network, had to be moved over, if possible. They could compete. Heroin affected the user much differently than cocaine—cocaine excited the user, then, after a short period of exhilaration, let him crash to the floor, while heroin was much longer lasting and gave a sense of euphoria, which cushioned the fall. Heroin could also be injected using number four, or inhaled or smoked using number three.

Tong leaders in Chinese settlements in nearly every major city in the world would be invited to apply for participation, or at least cooperation. And, of course, there could be no refusal.

Shipping lanes and distribution centers were selected. At first, the highest purity China White number four was promoted throughout the world. Here in the United States, the drug began showing up in the entertainment centers of Los Angeles and New York. Speedballing (injecting a mixture of cocaine and heroin) was introduced and became an instant success and soon became widely used from coast to coast. Heroin consumption was on the rise.

In San Francisco, the Wo Hop To, under the leadership of Peter "Uncle" Chong, was aggressively pushing the China White. In the city, the self indulgences of the affluent were running into a strange check and balance put out by nature—AIDS. People were scared. Slamming drugs into a vein could result in a penalty of death if the needle was contaminated. Then Chong discovered a new slant. Why not smoke the heroin? Heroin number three was smokable and effective. This less-than-pure heroin became touted as a "safe" drug. Now the user had access to an abundant supply of heroin that could be smoked or snorted. Many users became believers and gave up cocaine.

Peter Chong then enlisted the aid of Raymond "Shrimp Boy" Chow, a member of the Hop Sing Tong, who became a lieutenant with the Wo Hop To to help spread the criminal enterprise across the United States. A unique part of triad membership among ethnic Chinese is that the member who has been accepted and initiated into a triad can, if he so desires, leave the parent triad and apply for membership in a different one. This is usually done because the member feels his opportunities may be better in a different triad. Chow recruited about 100 Asian gangsters to help in the importation and distribution of heroin eastward to New England. This all came to an abrupt end in October 1993 when the federal government brought racketeering charges against Chong, Chow, and Wayne "Fat Boy" Kwong, the reputed leader of the On Leong Triad of Massachusetts. The 48 count RICO (Racketeer Influenced and Corrupt Organization) indictment named 19 reputed gang members, who are being charged with crimes ranging from loan-sharking, arson, robbery, murder, and drug smuggling.

Chow fled to Hong Kong and was arrested there and jailed awaiting extradition. In February 1995, Chow was back in San Francisco fighting his case in court.

CHARACTERISTICS OF ASIAN GANG MEMBERS

Some Asian gang member identifiers are as follows.

- Asian gang members are usually slight in stature, but may be buffed from working out with weights.
- Many are proficient in the marital arts.
- Their ages range from 12 years up through the 20s.
- They wear punk or new wave hair styles. They may change their identity by dyeing their hair with a washable dye, which is easy to remove after committing a robbery or other crime.
- They are beginning to stake out their turf using graffiti.
- Hand signs are used.
- Tattoos consist of snakes, tigers, lions, sailing ships, dragons, and the names or initials of the gang. A typical Bahala Na tattoo is "BNG—?" This translates into, "Whatever happens, happens." Chinese gang members like to tattoo phrases like, "Don't fuck with me," "I walk on water," and "T T T T T" (five Ts), which stand for Tinh

(Love), Tien (Money), Tu (Prison), Toi (Sin), and Thu (Revenge).
- Many have cigarette burns on the hands, faces, and other open areas. This is usually the result of their proving their ability to stand up to pain.
- Many carry false identification, and, if of legal age, they may use identification purporting to show them as minors.

ASIAN STREET GANG TERMINOLOGY

The Box: Jail.
Cowboy: Vietnamese name for criminal.
Cung: Marijuana.
Dal-Low: Big brother; leader or senior of group.
FBI: Plain-clothes officer.
Gangster: Vietnamese name for criminal who uses a gun.
Go Hop: Going to jail.
Green Paper: Money.
Home Boy: Asian youth who stays home, out of trouble.
Los: Los Angeles.
Mo: Motel.
One Eye: Car with only one headlight.
Party Lights: Light bar on a patrol car.
Pix: Lock picks.
Play: Committing crime.
Rocking: Cooking cocaine into rock.
School Boy: Asian youth who attends school regularly.
White: Cocaine.
Yim-Jai 25: Snitch.

7 ▶ Colombian Gangs

In Bogota, Colombia, on March 12, 1994, Julio Fabio Urdinola, a leader of one of Colombia's largest cocaine trafficking gangs, was taken into custody. Urdinola surrendered to authorities after months of negotiations by his lawyers. A reputed leader of the Cali Cartel, Urdinola turned himself in just 100 days after the military hunted down and killed Pablo Escobar, boss of the Medellin Cartel. U.S. officials were worried that the Colombian government would be lenient with Urdinola because a recently passed law granted leniency to traffickers who surrender, disclose their operation, and turn over to the government all of their illicit gains.

For years, Colombia has been the base of operations for four major drug cartels: the Medellin, the Cali, the Bogota, and the North Coast Cartel. The Medellin has been the major front-runner, with distribution operations in many of the largest U.S. cities. The Cali Cartel, with distribution centers in California, New York, Florida, Massachusetts, and New Jersey, has not been far behind.

The Medellin Cartel has been the organization heard from most often because of the trail of blood and violence it has left in its wake. Informers, competitors, debtors, and, most importantly, civic officials have been slain by members of the Medellin Cartel, who look upon murder and savagery as a necessary part of doing business. The term *magnicidio* (assassination of an important person) is used by the Medellin Cartel to instill fear into the populace and keep it in line. And this ruthlessness has not been confined only to Colombia. In 1986, while under federal protection in Louisiana, drug informant Barry Seal was gunned down by cartel hit men. During the Dade County cocaine wars of 1979 through 1982, 250 persons were killed in South Florida as cartels fought over distribution rights. Wives and children of gang members were slain along with the husbands and fathers. Innocent bystanders, who happened to be in the wrong place at the wrong time, were also gunned down. And amid this carnage, members of the U.S. judiciary received numerous death threats.

Many other persons have been corrupted by the drug cartels. U.S. law enforcement officers, including men and women of the Drug Enforcement Agency (DEA), Customs, Miami Police Department, Border Patrol, Federal Bureau of Investigations (FBI), and LAPD, as well as assistant U.S. attorneys have been caught up in the web of narcotics and apprehended on charges of cooperating with drug dealers in the sale and distribution of Colombian processed cocaine.

Prior to the explosive demand for Colombian cocaine, illegal activities in that country primarily included smuggling emeralds and other precious gems into the United States and teaching the art of pickpocketing at sophisticated schools. The School of the Seven Bells, so named because the bells attached to the instructor/victim's clothes sounded whenever the less-than-adept student practiced using too heavy a hand, was located in Bogota and considered its graduates to be the finest pickpockets in the world.

THE CELL SYSTEM

The Colombian cartels use the cell system within their organizations. The purpose of using this type of system is to eliminate contact between as many of the cartel operatives as possible. This has obvious advantages. When a lower echelon worker is arrested, his knowledge of the organization is limited, as is the information acquired by informants or others who have the potential to inform.

The cell system is nothing more than a team organized under a Colombian-based manager. The members of one team—or cell—have little or no contact with other cell members. Thus, any cell member would be hard pressed to identify a member of another cell or to describe the other cell's criminal activity. And to carry it further, few, if any, of the lower echelon workers would be able to identify any of the cartel's higher officers.

The Colombian drug lords utilize two unattached cell system structures. One is a cartel-based, organized structure that has tentacles reaching halfway around the world and back again to the home office in Colombia. All the cell managers and other important cell workers are members of this cartel. The second structure is formed around reliable and proven independent contractors. These independents have no family ties to the cartel but have proven to be quite capable and dependable. These independent cell managers maintain contacts within the cartel's hierarchy and enter into contracts with the cartel. Usually, these contracts are for a specific assignment. These assignments may be anything from the sale and distribution of a large quantity of cocaine to the laundering of a sizable amount of money. The independent contractor who accepts this type of contract assembles his own cell and recruits his own people. These temporary cell workers are usually paid a certain amount of money for their work, and after the operation has been completed, fade back into their own murky world.

Many of these independent contractors are free to contract with competing cartels once their current work assignment is completed. Thus, during the first part of a year, they may be responsible for transporting and warehousing an extra large shipment of cocaine for the Medellin Cartel, and during the second half of the year, they may be engaged in distributing and selling Cali cocaine. This further confuses the

DEA investigators and those of other government agencies who are trying to establish family ties or other recognizable traits during the course of an investigation.

Experts in the field estimate that there may be as many as 300 drug trafficking cells operating within the United States. Some of the smaller cells may have only a few members; others may have as many as 40 to 50. Many of these cell managers will use housewives, retired persons, students, and other laypeople to courier their drugs and money. This further complicates the efforts of the investigators, who may be looking for the classical drug runner profile. The cell managers also practice strict countersurveillance tactics to keep from being followed or surprised by the authorities or competing cartels. Countersurveillance tactics are taught by independent organizations nationwide and include seminars on eluding pursuers in traffic, the use of police scanners, defensive weaponry, the use of crash cars, and the use of safe houses, among other topics. One merely has to pick up any of the soldier-of-fortune type magazines available anywhere to learn the names and locations of these training centers.

COCAINE

Most of the coca leaf that ends up in Colombian labs is grown in Bolivia and Peru and, to a lesser extent, in Ecuador and Colombia. The leaves of the bush are harvested three to four times a year. During harvest, the leaves are processed into crude coca paste and from there are transported to Colombian laboratories to be converted into cocaine hydrochloride. The dense jungles of Colombia provide the ideal cover for the hidden laboratories and airfields needed in cocaine manufacture and distribution. An estimated 250,000 persons are employed in the Colombian cocaine industry. A typical laboratory may cover scores of acres with facilities for the employees that include dormitories, a culinary, retail stores, repair garages, quarters for the security troops, and the ever-present airfield and hangers. Gasoline storage is also close at hand.

In the processing labs, volatile chemicals such as acetone, ether, and hydrochloric acid are used in the conversion of the paste into cocaine HCL. To process one kilo of cocaine requires the use of 17 liters of ether. In Colombia, the sale of these chemicals is now controlled by the government, and as a result, the prices have risen sharply. Black marketeers have moved in to assist the cocaine manufacturers. This removes the threat of a paper trail attached to the cartels that ensues when buying the chemicals legally. However, this does nothing to keep the prices down. (A 55-gallon drum of ether that sells for $400 in the United States sells for approximately $10,000 on the Colombian black market.) As a result, the cartels have begun to establish laboratories across the border in neighboring Venezuela and in Ecuador, where the chemicals can be purchased at a much lower cost. Also, some sources insist that the Colombian cartels have recently established processing labs in the United States.

Prices on the refined cocaine available in the United States vary, but a kilo of the white powder with a purity of 85 to 95 percent currently wholesales for somewhere near $20,000. When this kilo is stepped on and reduced to about 55 percent purity and then packaged in gram-sized bindles and sold on the streets to the army of addicts in waiting, its value approaches $200,000. Back in Bolivia, the cocaine farmer who supplied the 250 to 500 kilos of leaves required to produce this one kilo of coke was paid $500 for his effort.

MEDELLIN CARTEL

In Medellin, an Andean tourist city of some 1.5 million people, about 20 families make up the largest cocaine cartel in the world: the Medellin Cartel. The estimated worth of these families totals billions of dollars. The cartel is structured much like a Wall Street conglomerate, with its highest ranking officers overseeing the base of operations that include laboratories, transportation (air, ground, and sea), warehousing and distribution, money laundering, enforcement, protection, investments, bribery, and all related divisions and subdivisions. In addition to the structured illegitimacy of the cocaine network, hundreds of millions of dollars are poured into legitimate businesses.

The nation itself has a recent history of violent death through civil wars, strife, and now drug trafficking. During the civil war of 1948 through 1958—La Violencia—the death toll amounted to about 300,000 persons. Today, Columbia has a murder rate of approximately 59 per 100,000 people; in comparison, the United States has a rate of 11 persons killed per 100,000. This acceptance of violent death by the average Colombian is reflected in their everyday life. Professional assassins are trained in a technique known as *asesino de la moto*. The rider of a motorbike, armed with a powerful weapon such as a MAC-11, rides up to the victim, who is taken by surprise, quickly shoots and kills him, and then disappears in a cloud of dust.

The Medellin's hit squads operate worldwide when necessary to enforce the precepts set down by the cartel. Torture and mutilation are tools they frequently use. In 1982, in New York City, a 32-year-old Colombian, an illegal alien and drug dealer who had apparently fallen out of favor with the cartel, was found slumped over in his Mercedes, shot to death by the cartel's hit squad. In his apartment, police discovered an arsenal of weapons, 140 pounds of cocaine, and close to a million dollars in cash. Also, the body of his wife, his 18-month-old daughter, and his 4-month-old son were found. They, too, had been slain by the hit squad shooters. Acts of this sort have served notice on the cartel's enemies and competitors that the Colombians intend to preserve their empires—and will do so in a sea of blood if necessary, without hesitation.

Carlos Lehder-Rivas
Lehder-Rivas was born in Colombia in 1949 of a Colombian mother and a German father. During his early

teens, the family broke up, and his mother took him out of Colombia to the United States. They settled in Detroit, where he learned the English language and American ways. He soon became part of a street gang specializing in stealing cars. He was eventually arrested for auto theft and released on bail pending trial. While out on bail, Lehder-Rivas skipped and was picked up three months later in Florida in possession of 237 pounds of marijuana.

Next stop was the federal prison in Danbury, Connecticut, where he made new criminal contacts, including a friendship with an inmate named George Jung, a small-time pot dealer and student activist. Jung had been supplying drugs to the Hollywood crowd and had connections in the film and record industries.

Lehder-Rivas was let out of prison in 1975 and deported to Colombia. Two years later, however, he again surfaced in the United States and made contact with his former inmate buddy George Jung. Lehder-Rivas had lined up contacts within the Medellin Cartel, and he and Jung formulated a plan to flood the United States with Colombian cocaine. Lehder-Rivas would line up stooges to smuggle the coke in using suitcases, and Jung would market the product in California. The scheme was an instant success. Money poured in.

Before long, the two cocaine entrepreneurs were bringing the product in by private plane. America was becoming addicted. Lehder-Rivas and Jung became millionaires; the Medellin Cartel was in full swing. In 1978, Lehder-Rivas moved to Norman's Cay in the Bahamas. He invested in an aircraft company and airstrip, a hotel, a yacht club and marina, and a lavish home. And of course he stepped up his cocaine smuggling pursuits.

He continued to prosper and allegedly had many of the Bahaman officials on the take. He maintained a close working relationship with Pablo Escobar and Jorge Ochoa, two of the Medellin's top echelon. In 1981, the U.S. government built up a substantial case against Lehder-Rivas and issued a warrant for his arrest on drug trafficking and income tax evasion charges. Lehder-Rivas left everything and headed back to Colombia.

On Colombian television, Lehder-Rivas denounced America and vowed to continue sending drugs into the United States as a weapon against North American imperialism. His messages had taken on a distinct anti-American overtone. He also founded a Nazi type youth movement patterned after the Hitler youth movement of the 1930s. He called this organization Los Lenadores—The Woodcutters. It may have been that Lehder-Rivas had become even too hot for the Medellin Cartel to control, or it may have been only coincidence (some sources insist he was informed on by his own people), but he was hunted down by Colombian authorities and captured in a shoot-out in 1987. He was then extradited to the United States to await trial.

On July 20, 1988, the federal trial of Carlos Lehder-Rivas was concluded. He was acknowledged to be the engineer behind the first large-scale cocaine smuggling system responsible for introducing the illegal drug into the United States. He was convicted of the importation of 3.3 tons of cocaine into this country and sentenced to a life term plus 135 years to be served in a U.S. federal prison, where he languishes today.

CALI CARTEL

Cali, a city of about 1 million persons, lies approximately 200 miles south of Medellin. The city is a major transportation, industrial, and commercial center for the Cauca River valley, where sugarcane, coffee, tobacco, cotton, cacao, bananas, rice, and corn are grown. It is also a livestock center where cattle and hogs are raised. Coal mining is extensive. With a large labor pool of *campesinos* at hand, the heavy jungle foliage, and the availability of the necessary supplies, the area is well suited for the importation of the coca paste and its conversion into cocaine HCL in hidden jungle labs. The rail centers and closeness to the seaport of Buenaventura further encourage the illegal production and distribution of the drug.

As the Medellin Cartel became deeply involved in cocaine trafficking, several powerful families in Cali copied them and formed the Cali Cartel. The Cali people soon claimed trafficking rights in New York City, Miami, and other U.S. cities already under siege by the Medellin gangsters. An uneasy truce between the two cartels fell apart in 1987 when they became engaged in violent warfare over the distribution rights of the drug in New York. The war exploded in New York and Florida and also back in Colombia, where each side enlisted its own soldiers to fight the other. Indiscriminate bombings claimed innocent as well as cartel-connected lives. Things eventually subsided, although flare-ups occur without notice.

Where the Medellin Cartel has been responsible for slaying countless police officers, government officials, supreme court justices, and other public officials, the Cali Cartel leaders have tried to stay away from this approach, preferring to subvert these public officials with bribes and other payoffs. This strategy has worked for the Cali people in that they have gained many loyal supporters throughout the country and have not accrued the rosters of enemies that have plagued the Medellin gangsters.

This strategy has also been used to corrupt U.S. officials, though it has not always been successful. In Chicago, in 1989, 29 Colombians affiliated with four of the Cali Cartel families were indicted on charges of running a multimillion-dollar drug ring responsible for dealing up to 440 pounds of cocaine a month in the Chicago area. The ring was said to have been operating out of four jewelry stores located on the north side of the city.

8 ▶ The Cuban Marielito

IN APRIL 1980, AT MARIEL HARBOR, CUBA, THE FIRST OF 125,000 Cuban refugees assembled a ragged collection of boats and ships and set sail for Miami 90 miles away and what they hoped would be a new life in a new world. Fidel Castro had finally given permission for these Cubans to leave the island. Most were legitimate Cuban citizens who were fed up with Castro and his brand of Marxism. Others were undesirables from Cuban prisons and mental institutions.

In Florida, they were whisked away into processing centers and holding areas while the government tried to determine their status. The federal government, at that time headed by President Jimmy Carter, bounced the Cubans' status back and forth through the courts until a federal judge decided that they were, in reality, applicants for asylum rather than refugees. In June, a presidential order further paved the way for the Cubans when they were granted entrant status. This effectively made them eligible for further assistance such as work permits, Aid to Dependent Children, Medicaid, Social Security, and other welfare programs.

The Cubans who were suspected felons were placed in federal prisons and other correctional facilities. The United States wanted to send them back to Cuba, but the Cuban government refused to accept them. To complicate matters, in January 1981, federal Judge Richard D. Rodgers ruled that the Cubans now being held in U.S. prisons could not be held indefinitely without charges or hearings. By the end of the year, nearly 1,000 of those being held under this statute were ordered released. They were subsequently freed and migrated to many of the United States' fast-paced cities and joined other Cubans already engaged in illegal street crime. Most of these Cuban criminals had been imprisoned in Cuba and had sailed from Mariel Harbor during the boat lift. They took great pride in referring to each other as Marielitos—not Cubans. Cubans were the squares.

Many of these Marielitos had also served time in the Cuban army and seen combat in Angola and other unstable countries. They were, for the most part, heavily tattooed, clever, devious, skilled at weaponry, and had become hardened to killing and life in prison. They welcomed violence as a means to achieve rapid wealth and status. Drug trafficking, murder, armed robberies, auto theft and chop shop operations, commercial burglaries, and upper echelon drug rip-offs were the necessary means used to acquire all that America had to offer. And they were very good at what they did. They preferred heavy caliber automatic and semiautomatic weapons and shunned smaller caliber Saturday Night Specials. They used crash cars to stop the police while evading arrest. If they were unlucky enough to get caught, which is what happened to many of them, they regarded the U.S. jails and prisons as soft compared to what they had experienced back home. In spite of the incarceration rate of these criminals, estimates as to the numbers of these Marielitos operating on the streets of America run as high as 40,000—out of an estimated 125,000 that came over on the flotilla.

In the U.S. prisons, they have been well behaved at times, but at other times they have caused millions of dollars in damage to our prisons, such as during the Cuban riot in the Atlanta federal penitentiary, when they went on a rampage of destruction. Still, they have shown restraint by harming very few prison staff members. A Cuban-American prisoner who has served time with them had this to say: "They came originally out of anti-Marxist Cuban families and were jailed when very young for minor complaints. But you must understand that underneath everything with them, there is this anti-Americanism of the Marxists. They think they have the right to do anything here. They resent the freedom and they don't know what to do with it.

"They call themselves 'Marielitos,' not Cubans. They identify themselves through the Mariel experience. That gave them their form. They call people outside 'civilians'—by inversion, they identify themselves as military. They feel that nobody can touch them—they're 'Marielitos.'"

Tattooing is regarded as a vulgar practice by the law-abiding Cuban population. However, among the Cuban criminals it is thought of as a sign of status. Most of the Cubans that were imprisoned in Cuba are tattooed, ranging from domino dots on the web of the hand (that denote a specific criminal expertise) through profane writing on the inside of the lips to large religious figures (Babalu-Aye and Santa Barbara, for example) adorning the back. Block letters that spell out Santeria (an Afro-Cubano religion that engages in animal sacrifice) or words such as Cuban Mafioso across the abdomen have also been seen. American Indian heads are seen frequently, as are mermaids.

Cuban Marielitos imprisoned in the United States are boisterous. They converse in loud, harsh tones, play their radios loud, and yell from cell to cell. Some of the correctional officers who are not familiar with them don't understand this part of their culture and are prone to push the panic button over what the Cubans consider to be normal.

Many of the Cubans imprisoned in the United States have proven to be very skillful and con wise in adapting to life in our prisons. They are excellent at fashioning weapons, lock picks, and other items of contraband out of materials easily accessible in prisons. One inmate used a one-gallon-sized culinary can placed over a fire on the floor of his cell to heat and melt plastic knives, forks, and spoons saved over from his meals. Out of the melted plastic, he was able to make var-

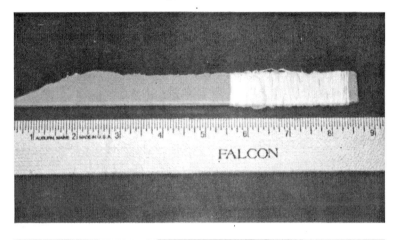

FALCON

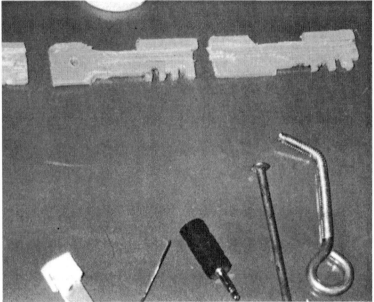

These are examples of Cuban Marielito prison craftsmanship. The first photo shows a shank, approximately 8 1/2 inches in length. The second photo shows Folger-Adams type keys. The shank and keys, all heavy plastic, were made from pieces of the footlocker in the prisoner's cell. Nylon thread taken from the mattress was used to cut and shape the items.

ious weapons, including knives and other items as harmless as hair barrettes.

Another Cuban prisoner removed lengths of the strong nylon thread holding his mattress together and used it as one would use dental floss to cut thick, blank pieces of plastic approximately 10 to 12 inches long and two inches wide from his footlocker, which he then used to make weapons and a number of Folger-Adams type keys. When discovered, the keys proved to be capable of opening the strong, barred gates in the cell block.

9 ▶ Hell's Angels

CURRENTLY, THERE ARE AN ESTIMATED 500 ACTIVE BIKER GANGS operating in the United States. Unquestionably, the richest and the best organized is the Hell's Angels. The other most important biker gangs are the Pagans, the Bandidos, and the Outlaws. They are all involved in drug manufacture and sales and other criminal activities, ranging from weapons trafficking to providing false identities. Lesser regional biker gangs work alongside these big four.

The Hell's Angels (HAs) motorcycle club had their beginning in San Bernardino, California, not long after the end of World War II. The founders, for the most part, were World War II veterans, malcontents on the edge of society, and other antisocial types who just wanted to raise hell. From the very start, their behavior, mode of dress, and disregard for the law drew the indignation of the straight public.

In an era when hundreds of thousands of American families had seen close relatives sacrificed on bloody European battlefields at the hands of the Nazis, the Hell's Angels rubbed salt into the wounds of the post-war survivors by incorporating the swastika, iron cross, and other Nazi insignia into the biker lifestyle here at home. The biker's clubhouse, personal adornments, and tattoos reflected Nazism. They were seen as antisocial racists, misfit lawbreakers, and barroom brawlers. They were to become the role models for all other outlaw bikers to follow. The HAs set the standards.

The Early Years

The HAs began to make themselves known in the 1950s. They gained notoriety when they roared into smaller towns and menaced the local inhabitants and intimidated under-staffed sheriff's departments. Law enforcement began taking a hard look at the activities of the Angels, and select officers in some departments were assigned full time to gather and disseminate intelligence on the outlaw bikers. In 1957, Sonny Barger, from Modesto, California, and fresh out of the army, joined the Angels. Barger brought something to the club that had been lacking from the start: the ability to organize. A year later, the 20-year-old Barger became the club's president. He began to structure the club and set out to establish a foundation that it could build on. The mother chapter was moved from San Bernardino to Oakland, and sanction chapters were planned for other California cities. New members were screened carefully.

The colors are emblazoned on the back of the jacket, which includes the name of the club and the Hell's Angels name, riding above the winged death's head. Below this, the rocker identifies the chapter, in this case, the Berdoo (San Bernardino) chapter.

Recruits were plentiful; it seemed there were wannabe outlaw biker types everywhere. Many were accepted, while others were told to hit the road. The use of human waste in their initiation ceremonies helped to advance the image they wanted to project: one of raucousness. Feces, urine, semen, and sewage became part of a prospect's colors—the jacket and official emblem of the biker gang—which could never be cleaned or washed. The original colors (red and white), the Hell's Angels name, the winged death's head, and the rocker naming the member's chapter were emblazoned on the back of their jackets. With one or two exceptions, these colors have changed little in the more than 40 years of the club's existence.

Hollywood Gets Into the Act

The media stepped up its coverage, and Hollywood ground out cheap movies trying to glamorize the bikers. In an attempt to upgrade the image of motorcycling, the American Motorcycle Association, a legitimate organization, embarked on an ad campaign declaring the outlaw bikers as nothing more than that—outlaws. The biker outlaws, they said, comprised only 1 percent of the population that enjoyed motorcycling. Ninety-nine percent of those riding bikes were law-abiding citizens. The HAs jumped on that right away. They took pride in being labeled one-percenters. It gave them a sought-after sense of identity. Soon their colors, their tattoos, and their sense of belonging were all ingrained into the one-percenter concept. One-percenter patches became a part of their colors.

During the 1960s, Hollywood continued to ride the notoriety of the club. Barger became a paid advisor and part-time actor for film companies that were making movies about outlaw bikers. In 1967, he had a role with Jack Nicholson in *Hell's Angels On Wheels*. He also consulted with several authors who were writing books or articles about the gang.

Expansion

The club membership increased dramatically as other outlaw biker gangs buried their own colors and joined the Hell's Angels. Entire clubs were absorbed into the HAs. Many prospects were considered unsuitable and sent on their way. The HAs were also beginning to pile up money, yet in the mid-60s, the club was nearly bankrupt; legal fees had all but wiped out the treasury. Many of the gang members held down steady jobs, while others lived by their wits, many by dealing in stolen bikes and bike parts. The club occasionally was hired to provide security at rock concerts. In 1966, they incorporated and issued shares. Their colors—the winged death's head—received a U.S. patent. Still, they were close to dissolution. Most sources say this is when they entered full scale into drug trafficking and became the number one manufacturer and supplier of methamphetamine (crank). They also expanded their other illegitimate enterprises: gunrunning, prostitution, truck hijacking, gambling, forgery, robbery, extortion, assault, and auto and motorcycle theft.

As the club entered into the 1970s, they had chapters not only in California but in the Midwest, New York, New England, Canada, New Zealand, and England.

Barger Goes to San Quentin

In 1973, Sonny Barger went to prison for drug sales. The club continued its expansion. In 1977, Barger was paroled. The club had become mortal enemies with another outlaw biker gang called, quite appropriately, the Outlaws. By the time Barger was released from prison, members of the two biker gangs were killing each other on sight. Prospects for each club could gain membership at once if a kill against one of the other club's members was carried out.

Into the 1980s, the HAs had been investing heavily into legitimate businesses. They had also developed an underground network extending worldwide. Any one of their members on the run from the law could hide out indefinitely—in many different countries. They had begun to resemble traditional organized crime more than marauding bikers. Their New York chapters aligned with the Mafia, doing hits and other dirty work.

By 1990, they had chapters worldwide. Once a month there was an international meeting attended by all chapter presidents.

Organized Crime on Wheels

As they advance into the 1990s, the Hell's Angels are no longer a horde of beer guzzling misfits terrorizing small California towns. Instead, they are a highly structured, nationwide drug trafficking organization that controls most of the methamphetamine manufacture and distribution in the United States. They developed a working relationship with the Colombian cartels in order to deal cocaine in addition to meth. They also deal PCP and marijuana. Luxury automobiles have replaced Harleys. Three-piece suits have replaced scummy denim jackets. One thing remains: their reputation for ruthlessness.

The Hell's Angels have their own security forces, and they enforce their own internal discipline. Their technicians do their own polygraphs and voice stress analyses. Extensive background checks are done on all prospective members. Hell's Angels old ladies are discreetly put to work in telephone companies, prisons, police stations, courthouses, motor vehicle departments, and other sensitive areas to gather intelligence on law enforcement agencies, police officers and procedures, enemy gang members, and others. All incoming data is fed into computers, where it is stored and used within their own intelligence network. Their information banks rival those of many legitimate businesses.

Names of informers are sought out (this is one area where all biker gangs share information). Once identified, an informant is hunted down, tortured in order to learn what information he has revealed and to whom, and then disposed of. The body may be weighted down with concrete blocks and dumped into deep water or buried in remote deserts or mountains.

So many Hell's Angels members suspected of being informants have been killed upon orders of the club's officers that many others have rolled over and entered the Witness Protection Program. Here they hide out in uneasy protection, waiting until prosecutors can get them to court to testify. A high price is put on their heads by the HAs.

The Outlaws are still at war with the Angels. Their clubhouses stock explosives and automatic weapons to be used against their enemies when circumstances permit. They display banners that proclaim AHAMD (All Hell's Angels Must Die). Part of this hatred stems from fighting for control of the lucrative illegal drug market, chiefly methamphetamine.

Methamphetamine

Methamphetamine, a synthetic drug, has been produced in local laboratories for many years under the supervision of journeymen cookers on the Angels' payroll. The cooks must use sophisticated pressure hydrogenators along with hydrogen gas, tanks, beakers, lines, and a series of pressured gauges in formulating the drug. The necessary chemicals include highly caustic acids, oils, alcohols, and ether. Working in this kind of a setting is extremely dangerous; the volatile fumes generated may explode unexpectedly, and pressurized lines may rupture, enveloping the area in clouds of poisonous gases that are not only toxic to the skin but deadly if inhaled. Accomplished cooks are sought after and paid well for their expertise.

When done right, the finished product is a white, highly addictive powder—a central nervous system stimulant—that can be injected, snorted, or ingested and is in great demand in the United States and scores of foreign countries. With their network now stretching to the far corners of the world, the outlaw bikers are able to distribute the "crank" worldwide. Japan is one of their highly lucrative meth markets.

Crystal Methamphetamine

In 1987, a new form of meth rose like a specter from hid-

den Asian laboratories and exploded ferociously upon the shores of Hawaii. Asian chemists developed "ice," a rock-like form of methamphetamine that could be smoked and gave an instant, long-lasting high. The Hawaiian Islands were targeted to be the first state to offer U.S. citizens this new alternative to cocaine addiction. Cocaine had become the rich man's drug of choice, and even in the ghetto, many crackheads had built up $400- to $500-a-day habits smoking crack. But now, with the advent of this new drug, the street-level addicts could hit, get high, and stay there for a long time for a lot less money. Law enforcement recoiled under the weight of gearing up for this new invasion, and intelligence gathering resources stepped up surveillance to learn what part the Angels would play in all this.

Ice closely resembles rock salt or rock candy in appearance, but that is where the similarity ends. It is a dangerous drug that may look pretty but has proven to be lethal to many users. In Hawaii, it is known as *batu*. On the streets of the mainland, it is known as ice, or "crystal."

Unlike street meth that usually has been stepped on repeatedly before reaching the consumer, crystal meth is nearly 98 to 100 percent pure. Many addicts are switching to ice because it's cheaper than crack cocaine and gives a much longer high. When a hit of ice is smoked, it may reward the user with a high that lasts up to 12 hours. This is in marked contrast to crack, which gives the addict only a brief high lasting a few minutes. Costwise, ice again scores first. One hit, one-tenth of a gram, sells in the neighborhood of $50. A gram, enough for 10 to 25 hits, sells for anywhere between $250 to $400. An ounce sells for around $7,000.

Ice burns much cooler than crack cocaine, and the smoking pipes, or bongs, are distinctly different. Ice bongs use no screen or cooling section. Most are simple, one-piece objects made of glass with a central heating chamber, a vent hole (called a carb), and a mouthpiece. The crystal is placed directly into the main heating chamber and heated from the bottom of the bong using a lighter. The carb is covered with

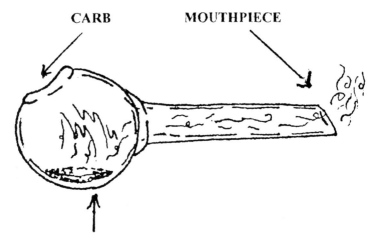

CARB   MOUTHPIECE

MAIN HEATING CHAMBER

Bong for smoking crystal meth (ice).

the finger and the meth quickly becomes a gas, which is then inhaled through the mouthpiece.

IDENTIFICATION OF OUTLAW BIKERS

Colors

It is difficult to mistake an outlaw biker if he is wearing his colors: dirty jeans, jack boots, and Levi's type denim jackets (sometimes sleeveless) or leather jackets with the club emblem splashed across the back. One-percenter patches and Nazi emblems, such as the iron cross and swastika, are seen frequently.

Tattoos

Most hard-core members will be covered with ink, displaying a multitude of tattoos. With the Hell's Angels, look for the winged death's head tattoo and the letters MC (motorcycle club). The club name spelled out may be present

Colors are the jacket and official emblem of the biker gang.

A tattoo of winged death's head.

The wings, a patch or metal pin, are worn on the front of the jacket to announce the sexual prowess of the wearer.

as well as the letters HA, or sometimes the letters AJ (AJ spoken rapidly sounds like HA).

The true executioners of the Hell's Angels are authorized to wear the enforcer's tattoo, the words "Filthy Few" atop the Nazi-style SS. Occasionally, a renegade biker has been caught wearing an unauthorized tattoo. After a severe beating, the tattoo is removed along with the skin.

Wings

Wings are patches of cloth or metal affixed to the colors. Wings denote sexual deviations.

Golden: Participation in a gang bang involving more than 15 men.
White: Performing cunnilingus on a white woman.
Red: Performing cunnilingus on a menstruating woman.
Black: Performing cunnilingus on a black woman.
Yellow: Performing cunnilingus on an Asian woman.
Green: Performing cunnilingus on a woman infested with insects.
Purple: Performing cunnilingus on a dead woman.
Brown: Performing analingus on a woman.

Blue and Yellow: Intercourse with a policewoman.
Eightball: Anal sex with a man in front of HAs.

Crosses

Crosses are worn as an earring, patch, or pin.

White: Earned for opening up a grave, taking something, and wearing the item as part of the colors.

Red: Performing fellatio on another male in front of HAs.

White Supremacists and Other White Gangs

DURING THE LAST DECADE, TENS OF THOUSANDS OF PEOPLE HAVE sold their homes and businesses in cities and relocated to the wilderness areas of the United States. They are fleeing what they believe to be an insensitive, oppressive federal government that they fear is stripping away their liberties one by one. They are also running away from what they consider to be an encroachment of nonwhite minorities, savage crimes being committed in the streets of their cities, and an inadequate criminal justice system. Most of these people share a belief in Christian doctrines, and many profess an obligation to preserve the white race. They are referred to as white supremacists.

THE ORDER

Bruce Pierce, an alleged member of the Order, a white supremacist organization, was serving multiple sentences in Leavenworth for armored car robberies and the murder of Denver talk show host Alan Berg. Earlier in the week, an inmate CI (confidential informant) had brought to the attention of the warden a bizarre escape plot said to be building involving both white and black inmates. The informant said that the blacks, members of the Black Liberation Army (BLA), had agreed to smuggle in guns, and the whites had the responsibility of lining up sharpshooters on the outside that would shoot and kill the lone officer manning the rear gun tower. Then, inmates would storm the tower and activate controls opening up the rear drive-through sally port. After that, waiting vans would complete the prisoners' escape.

This is, in essence, the story handed to the warden by the CI. And, as in all prisons, informants expect something in return for the dangerous game they play. After all, in prison a snitch is regarded as the lowest form of life. And they walk a perilous tightrope. Many times the informants divulge information that proves to be helpful to the administration; other times it is seen as pure baloney. In this case, however, the administration thought enough of the disclosure to act upon it immediately.

Pierce and his codefendant in the Berg killing, Richard Scutari, were swiftly moved out of Leavenworth and flown to the Federal Bureau of Prisons' maximum security penitentiary in Marion, Illinois. Inside Marion, the prisoners were locked up 23 hours a day, and whenever out of their cells, they were shackled hand and foot and moved under heavy guard.

Pierce and Scutari are representative of a growing number of white dissidents throughout the country that regard themselves as saviors of the white race. Both were members of the Order, also known as the Bruder Schweigen or Silent Brotherhood, a white supremacist organization headquartered in Metaline Falls, Washington.

The Order was founded in late 1983. The founders probably numbered fewer than a dozen initially and were led by a sensitive, middle class lumberjack named Robert Mathews. Mathews had been raised near Phoenix, Arizona, and early on joined the John Birch Society and a survivalist group known as the Sons of Liberty. He was active in right-wing politics and tax protester groups. He was eventually arrested and placed on probation for income tax fraud. He may have accepted probation as a more viable option than prison, but inside he seethed with bitterness. The seeds had been sown.

Mathews now had a mission, he reasoned, of establishing

a sanctuary where he and others could be free of the corruption and harassment of the federal government and the encroachment of minorities, especially blacks and Jews. He moved his family to the area around Hayden Lake, Idaho, the home of a long-standing white supremacist group called the Aryan Nation, where he was welcomed with open arms. He soon announced the formation of a whites-only church, the Church of Jesus Christ Christian. At last he felt at home and considered it his duty—or mission—to recruit other whites into the church to increase the ranks of the members and prepare for any eventuality, even if it meant leading the troops against the U.S. government. He soon had the nucleus of a dedicated vanguard ready to carve out a piece of Americana in the Pacific Northwest.

To finance their cause, they first tried clearing timber under a contract with the U.S. Forest Service. This idea went nowhere. After expenses and salaries were paid, little was left to finance any type of revolutionary action. What they needed was much more money in a much shorter time. They had been stockpiling arms since the inception of the movement, and now Mathews persuaded the others to put their weapons to work. Apparently, they all agreed. Their first stickup was in a Spokane porno shop that netted them $369 and the satisfaction of taking down what they considered to be a depraved symbol of a decaying country.

They quickly graduated from this nickel-and-dime beginning to a multistate crime spree that included armored car robberies and counterfeiting U.S. currency. Their take soon totaled millions of dollars. It is alleged they contributed heavily to other white supremacist groups.

From Armed Robbery to Murder

Alan Berg, a controversial Denver, Colorado, talk show host whose show was aired nightly, caught the attention of members of the Order with his liberal views. Berg spoke of white supremacist groups and anti-Semites as if they were a kind of plague. He also discussed his stance on gun control, and his caustic remarks directed at gun owners particularly infuriated members of the Order. At times, members of the group would call in to the show, only to be held up to ridicule by the slick-tongued ex-lawyer. Somewhere within the group, it was decided that ". . . the Jew would have to be killed."

And so it happened. On a warm June night in 1984, Berg had just pulled up in front of his Denver condo and prepared to exit the car when he was met by a hail of slugs fired from the silenced muzzle of a MAC-10. Bruce Pierce stepped out of the shadows and was met by Richard Scutari and another lookout. The three hopped into a getaway car, driven by a fourth member of the Order, and roared off into the night.

Berg's murder kicked off what the Order hoped would be the start of a series of assassinations directed at ZOG (Zionist Occupational Government). But the movement was doomed to fail. Internal dissension and the hot breath of the feds combined to forecast an end to the Order. Systematically, the members were hunted down and imprisoned.

Bob Mathews, the founder and acknowledged leader, was tracked to Whidbey Island, a 50-mile stretch of land on Puget Sound in Washington, where he had stockpiled survival supplies among three safehouses. On Saturday, December 8, 1984, more than 300 federal agents, along with local law enforcement officers, surrounded the house where Mathews was hiding. Then, all air and sea passage over and around the island was brought to a standstill. The feds ordered Mathews out of the house. When he elected to fight, a fierce gun battle erupted. In the end, Mathews was killed when the feds lit up the house using white phosphorous illumination flares.

Ultimately, 24 of the group's members were arrested and charged with crimes ranging from conspiracy to commit robbery to counterfeiting to murder. The resulting trials effectively destroyed what was left of the Order. However, much of the illegal money acquired by the Order was never found or accounted for. It was alleged that hundreds of thousands of dollars taken in armored car holdups was diverted to other white supremacist groups. Undoubtedly, it was. One, the White Patriot Party, a North Carolina-based group led by a former Green Beret, Glen Miller, was able to equip its troops with tens of thousands of dollars of new communications gear, uniforms, and weapons.

The Turner Diaries

The reign of the Order was short-lived and violent. The investigations and critical review hearings that were subsequently conducted by various governmental agencies concluded that the Order had actually taken its name from a white supremacist group of the same name, fictionalized in a book that had made the rounds of right-wing swap meets, mercenary and survivalist gatherings, and magazines that catered to soldier-of-fortune types. The book was *The Turner Diaries*.

The Turner Diaries was written in 1978 by a former Oregon State University physics professor, William Pierce (no relation to Bruce Pierce). William Pierce had been a one-time publicist for George Lincoln Rockwell, the American Nazi leader. He later went on to found another neo-Nazi group, the National Alliance.

In the book, the protagonist leads members of the Order on a mission of terror and lynching of blacks, Jews, and other minorities and the white women who bedded with and married them. Many of the far-right extremist groups regarded *The Turner Diaries* as their bible. It undoubtedly had a great influence on the scholarly appearing Bob Mathews.

ARYAN NATIONS

The Aryan Nations traces its roots back 60 years through Ku Klux Klan affiliation, varied leadership, geographical movement, and the Christian Identity movement. In the 1960s, the organization settled in the area of Hayden Lake, Idaho, where it built a church school and a paramilitary staging area on 20-some acres. Under the leadership of Richard

The logo and emblem of the Aryan Nations.

Butler, the compound opened with more than 100 adherents, initially, with scores of other Aryan racists following.

Butler recruited energetically and welcomed ex-felons that had been aligned with the Aryan Brotherhood while in prison. AB members schooled in prison were usually heavily tattooed, well-buffed from daily workouts with weights, well-connected with other white supremacists throughout the country, and prone to violence and hatred. In prisons where the AB have established chapters, the gang members are required to learn skills such as empty hand killing techniques, manufacturing explosives, weapon and handcuff key manufacturing, contraband concealment, knife fighting, baton takeaway techniques, and other necessary talents such as communication using the sign language of the hearing impaired.

The Aryan Nations encampment at Hayden Lake announced the first World Aryan Congress in 1982. White supremacists streamed into the gathering to exchange ideas on racial hatred, politics, governmental conspiracies against U.S. citizens, the World Bank, and related subjects. The meeting was successful in that it brought together dissidents of the far right from many different areas. It was to become an annual event.

By 1990, the yearly conference was drawing not only loosely structured skinheads and run-of-the-mill neo-Nazi types but organized hate groups such as the Ku Klux Klan, White Aryan Resistance (WAR), the antitax Posse Comitatus, the Werewolf Order of Southern California, and others. And many of those in attendance were wealthy, respected men of their communities.

The compound began to resemble a stalag type prison camp with barbed wire gun emplacements, Nazi-style swastikas and banners, and posters showing Hitler and other high-ranking Nazis. Indeed, April 20 of each year—Hitler's birthday—was observed as a holiday. Shaved-head youths stomping around with hob-nailed boots were seen throughout the meetings greeting each other with the Nazi salute. Weapons training and marksmanship matches were held in the forest under the watchful eye of skilled instructors, many of them Vietnam combat veterans. At the conclusion of each yearly conference, a ritualistic cross burning behind the compound's rear gun tower reminded all of those in attendance of their Christian Identity heritage and of their commitment to the preservation of the white race.

Aryan Nations Oath of Allegiance

"I, as a free Aryan man, hereby swear an unrelenting oath upon the green graves of our sires, upon the children in the wombs of our wives, upon the throne of God almighty, sacred is His name, to join together in holy union with those brothers in this circle and to declare forthright that from this

moment on I have no fear of death, no fear of foe, that I have a sacred duty to do whatever is necessary to deliver our people from the Jew and bring total victory to the Aryan race.

"I, as an Aryan warrior, swear myself to complete secrecy to the Order and total loyalty to my comrades.

"Let me bear witness to you, my brothers, that should one of you fall in battle, I will see to the welfare and well-being of your family.

"Let me bear witness to you, my brothers, that should one of you be taken prisoner, I will do whatever is necessary to regain your freedom.

"Let me bear witness to you, my brothers, that should an enemy agent hurt you, I will chase him to the ends of the earth and remove his head from his body.

"And furthermore, let me bear witness to you, my brothers, that if I break this oath, let me be forever cursed upon the lips of our people as a coward and an oath breaker.

"My brothers, let us be His battle-ax and weapons of war. Let us go forth by ones and twos, by scores and by legions, and as true Aryan men with pure hearts and strong minds face the enemies of our faith and our race with courage and determination.

"We hereby invoke the blood covenant and declare that we are in a full state of war and will not lay down our weapons until we have driven the enemy into the sea and reclaimed the land which was promised of our fathers of old, and through our blood and His will, becomes the land of our children to be."

White Aryan Resistance

The following is the text of a recorded phone message made available by Tom Metzger, leader of White Aryan Resistance (WAR) that claims a membership of more than 2,000.

"Almost all abortion doctors are Jews. Abortion makes money for Jews. Almost all abortion nurses are lesbians. Abortion gives thrills to lesbians. Abortion in Orange County

The logo and emblem of
White Aryan Resistance.

is promoted by the corrupt Jewish organization called
Planned Parenthood. The name alone proves their corruption
because they don't plan parents they plot the murder of
innocent white children. That organization gets money from
the State of California and corrupt payoffs from the lesbian
abortion clinics. Their administrators pay themselves high
salaries, and at the end of the day, they take the fetuses,
some of whom are still struggling for a breath of life, and
throw them in the garbage where the cats can eat them. They
can't stop now because when abortion is declared to be murder, they would be hung by piano wires for the holocaust of
20 million white children. Jews would do anything for
money, including the rape of innocent children, followed by

*the ripping and tearing of the living child from the young
mother's womb while it is still forming. Jews must be pun-
ished for this holocaust and murder of white children, along
with their perverted lesbian nurses who enjoy their work too
much. You have reached WAR . . . White Aryan Resistance."*

Metzger seems intent on a path of contradiction. A one-
time head of the California branch of David Duke's Ku Klux
Klan, Metzger broke away to form his own Klan "klavern" in
1981. In a speech made in 1980, he said, "You don't make
change having fiery crosses out in cow pastures. You make
change by invading the halls of Congress and the statehouse."
As a politician in 1982, he gathered 75,000 votes statewide in
the race for the Democratic nomination for the U.S. Senate.

Metzger is credited with getting his right-wing message
out to the youths of the country, resulting in large numbers
joining his movement and many others supporting his views
from the sidelines. WAR is reputed to have received millions
of dollars of stolen money from the Order to further the right-
wing cause.

Metzger has, on occasion, moved away from the right, as
he did when he couldn't sanction the views of those that supported a nuclear war with Russia. He felt it illogical to support
any effort that would result in the mass death of whites.

Ecological activists moved toward his organization after
the head of the Aryan Women's League wrote an article in
support of protecting wolves, as did Earth First people,
extremists who have been accused of spiking trees and have
made threats to sabotage power facilities.

In a Portland, Oregon, courtroom in October 1990,
Metzger was defending himself and WAR in a $10 million
lawsuit brought on by the family of a slain Ethiopian,
Mulugeta Seraw. Three skinheads, all members of the neo-
Nazi group East Side White Pride, had been convicted of
bludgeoning Seraw to death after Metzger allegedly told the
skinheads to "kick ass." "I tell the entire white working class
of this nation, figuratively and literally, that they are going to

A sampling of the literature put out by far-right hate groups.

have to kick ass just like our founding fathers did," Metzger said. "I make no apologies for that."

The courtroom procedures were carefully monitored daily by both racists and civil rights advocates sitting side by side. Ron Herndon, a black activist, stated, "Metzger symbolizes the rise of white hate groups in this country over the last 10 years. What happens to him will send a strong message one way or the other to the country."

Allegedly, two of Metzger's followers spoke to the attackers and encouraged violence hours before Seraw was slain. In an affidavit, Michael Barrett, one of the spokesmen, said they had brought five baseball bats to Portland with them and had held a meeting with the neo-Nazis. "Dave Mazzella and I told these skinheads that blacks and Jews were the enemy of the white Aryan race. We told them to use violence if they got the opportunity, and to be sure and beat the hell out of the enemy. We were telling them what Tom and John Metzger [his son] told us to say to skinheads we were organizing." Metzger lost the civil suit.

Metzger welcomes Christians and Christian Identity skinheads into his movement, yet he himself professes to be an atheist. He seems to be a master at attracting and recruiting youths into his organization, so much so that along with his son, John, he took over leadership of the Aryan Youth Movement (AYM), another white supremacist group, in 1987 when the founder, Greg Withrow, renounced racism.

SKINHEADS

Skinheads first appeared in the late 1960s in Great Britain. At first the trend appeared to be nothing more than youthful rebellion, part of which was directed against the Mods and hippie types of this era. The Mods were affluent, stylishly dressed youngsters that dominated the British rock-and-roll scene, and the hippies were permissive, submissive nonconformists. The young skinheads considered themselves working-class citizenry and resented the Mods and the hairy, raggedy hippies who seemed to have unlimited funds with which to frolic across Western Europe seeking excitement.

The skinheads were quick to develop their own identity: close-cropped hair, clean-shaven faces, tight jeans, button-down short-sleeve shirts, bomber jackets, narrow suspenders, and the most important accouterment, the high-topped, steel-toed, commando-style boots.

During the 1980s, as the skinhead ranks increased dramatically, hordes of immigrants were arriving daily. Pakistanis, West Indians, East Indians, Asians, and others disembarked and immediately started taking advantage of welfare and other benefits, including low-cost housing and medical care, that was paid for by British taxpayers. At this time, when unemployment was a grave concern, immigrants that were willing to work were accepting wages far lower than what the native-born would. This contributed to the loathing the skinheads held for the immigrants, which quickly developed into raw hatred.

Skinhead violence erupted. Baseball bats and steel-toed jackboots were their favorite weapons. These lethal boots were inevitably outlawed, but a substitute was soon found: Doc Martens. These boots were comfortable, sturdy, high-topped, could be shined to a high gloss, and had as many as 20 eyelets.

As other Western European countries struggled with the problem of rampant immigration during this time, the skinhead movement was moving across borders and oceans. In the United States, especially on the West Coast, skinheads attacked Asians and other nonwhites and desecrated Jewish cemeteries and synagogues. The U.S. and British skinheads, bound together by a common language and purpose, maintained close communication through newsletter, direct mail, and travel.

Greg Withrow

"*Some fathers raise their sons to be doctors, some fathers raise their sons to be lawyers. I was raised to be the Fuhrer.*"
—Greg Withrow

This skinhead banner depicts the bond between skinheads in the United Kingdom and the United States. The swastika in the center suggests the movement's identification with Nazi ideology.

Greg Withrow is credited with founding the skinhead movement in America. While Withrow was growing up, his father made him study the life of Hitler and read hate literature. At age 14, he joined the Ku Klux Klan (KKK), and later that same year he was arrested for mugging an undercover cop. "I had formed a racist group that went around mugging Japanese tourists and homosexuals. The cops set up decoys and I got arrested."

After serving a not-too-long jail term, he went to American River College in Sacramento and formed the White Student's Union and the Aryan Youth Movement. "We began making contact with skinheads in England, and we brought over the skinhead ideology," he said. "At first, many adult racists were not accepting of our movement, but in time they [skinheads] came to the forefront. They became the warriors. It became apparent that I held the youth movement in the palm of my hand.

"I called it the '100 Hitlers policy' to set up cells across the country. The police can crush one cell, two cells, but the movement continues." Leaders of the cells tend to meet each other only through more traditional organizations such as neo-Nazis, the Ku Klux Klan, and White Aryan Resistance, which use skinheads as foot soldiers, thus insulating the leaders and members of one cell from the others and protecting all members from informers and defectors.

Withrow knows first hand the movement's potential for violence. He said he decided to quit the movement in 1987 after his father died and he fell in love with a woman whose family had fled Hitler's Germany. She convinced him to renounce his racist ways. His former followers didn't take kindly to this turnaround. As he was leaving his apartment one night for a leisurely stroll, a fast-moving pickup truck screeched to a halt, and six skinheads jumped out and beat him into submission. They then dragged him into an empty lot and tied him to a board. Next, they nailed his outstretched hands to the board. As he lay writhing on the makeshift cross, one of the attackers carved a foot-long gash on his chest. Satisfied that they had made their statement, the six roared off in the pickup. Withrow survived and went on to become an accomplished kick boxer. Today, he supports himself by kick boxing and lecturing against white supremacy groups for the Anti-Defamation League.

During his frequent lectures, he tells his audience how his former best friend was one of the attackers: "I was attacked in a parking lot behind a K-Mart in Sacramento. My throat was cut in two places, my jaw was broken, my nose was broken, my head was cracked, my hands were nailed into a board like a crucifix, and I was told I would die like a Jew. They left me for dead."

Another white supremacist who renounced the movement was Tom Martinez. Martinez said he believes skinheads are the most dangerous segment of the hate movement. "There is a lot of angry youth out there," he said. "Many of these kids have a good gripe against society."

Fourth Reich Skinheads

In late July 1993, Christopher Fisher, 20, from Long Beach, California, and three of his followers were indicted by a federal grand jury on charges of manufacturing, possessing, and selling machine guns, silencers, and explosives. Fisher is alleged to be the leader of a violent white supremacist group known as the Fourth Reich Skinheads. This group is alleged to have ties to the Florida-based Church of the Creator and to the White Aryan Resistance.

The 20-count indictment accused the defendants of manufacturing Sten submachine guns, converting AR-15 assault rifles into fully automatic weapons, and manufacturing silencers. Other allegations included plotting to kill Rodney King, the black motorist involved in the trial of the four Los Angeles policemen in Simi Valley, throwing a Molotov cocktail at the window of a Westminster synagogue, and involvement in the pipe bomb attack of the home of a member of the infamous Spur Posse sex gang in suburban Lakewood. Other charges included plotting to bomb the First African Methodist Episcopal Church and plans to send out mail bombs to the Orange, California, Jewish community.

In a news conference, Danny Bakewell, a local black activist and president of the Brotherhood Crusade, identified himself as another target selected by the Fourth Reich Skinheads. To complicate matters, black gang members from South Central Los Angeles offered to defend Bakewell and also spoke of retaliation. "I have asked, 'Please do not resort to violence,'" Bakewell said. "I do not want this to become an opportunity for authorities to swoop down on our community."

FBI Special Agent Charlie Parsons said the plotters wanted to help start a race war. "That was their motivation," he added. "We prevented despicable and violent acts from occurring."

When contacted about the plot to kill him, Rodney King said, "I never feel safe, but this is one chapter in my life that I'd like to shut the door on. . . . We're wore out." If convicted, Fisher faces life in prison.

CHRISTIAN IDENTITY GROUPS

Most of the white separatist type persons profess to be affiliated with a Christian Identity church or movement. There are both. Many of the Christian Identity adherents have strong family ties and own homes, businesses, and other properties. One group can even point to one of their leaders as having run for president of the United States.

The Christian Identity Church

"Only Gritz can save America," followers declare. "The time is now—let's take America back!"

James "Bo" Gritz is a Nevada resident and former Green Beret lieutenant colonel who ran for president in 1992. He is a charismatic speaker and continuously hammers the government over Waco and the killing of Randy Weaver's wife and son (see below). Gritz says government officials involved in the siege in northern Idaho, as well as the more recent siege in Waco, Texas, should be prosecuted for the deaths in both places. "Somebody should stand trial," he said. Many people in the United States are in total agreement with him. A large portion of Gritz's followers are established family members, hard-working, law-abiding citizens who feel threatened by the increasingly oppressive government presence.

Gritz allegedly is a member of the Christian Identity church, the beliefs of which include white separatism. However, he insists that he also favors equality for non-whites. This church embraces portions of the Mormon, Baptist, and Christian Identity theologies. Gritz's followers include blue collar workers from the Pacific Northwest, racist skinheads, and activists against gun control. They want to see America withdraw from the United Nations, all foreign aid eliminated, a prohibition of foreign ownership of American properties and businesses, and an end put to the Internal Revenue Service, the Federal Reserve System, and the Department of Education. They want a stronger national defense, a weaker supreme court, and a Christian America. On February 20, 1994, it was reported that Bo Gritz and his associates purchased 280 acres of land near Kamiah, Idaho. Gritz denied accusations that he planned to use this land to open a boot camp for white supremacists.

The Christian Identity Movement

The tenets of the Christian Identity movement are similar to those of the Christian Identity church. It lists many churches among its following, which all enjoy a tax-exempt status. Some of them are, the Florida-based Church of the Creator, the Church of Jesus Christ Christian/Aryan Nations of Hayden Lake, Idaho, and the Church Universal Triumphant of Montana.

During the summer of 1992, Randy Weaver, a member of the Christian Identity movement, was involved in a bloody shoot-out with federal officers in a remote Idaho mountain cabin. With him were his wife, Vicky, their 14-year-old son, and another man, Kevin Harris. When the smoke cleared, Weaver's wife and son were dead, as was a U.S. Deputy Marshal, William Degan. Weaver and Harris still refused to surrender, and Bo Gritz flew in from Nevada in an attempt to talk the two men out of the cabin. He carried with him a letter addressed to Weaver from three skinheads. The strategy worked, and both men gave up. Inside the cabin, the U.S. Marshals found a poster of Gritz hanging on the wall.

The subsequent trial of Weaver and Harris for the murder of the Deputy Federal Marshal was held in Boise, Idaho, in June 1993. After a 20-day trial, the two men were acquitted of the murder charge, but Weaver was found guilty of two lesser charges. The jury was highly critical of the federal government's ill-prepared case. Sloppy investigative work, paranoia, and contradictory testimony by prosecution witnesses doomed the government's murder and conspiracy case against Randy Weaver and Kevin Harris, jurors said. Juror Janet Schmierer, a Boise electronics plant worker, said she was disturbed that agents of the FBI, the U.S. Marshals Service, and the BATF seemed bent on prosecuting people who hold unorthodox beliefs—the contention of the defendants' attorneys. "I think they built their whole scenario out of how they perceived someone else should be living their lives, and if someone believed differently from how (federal authorities) lived their lives, they must be abnormal," she said.

Jury foreman John Harris Weaver (no relation) was likewise critical: "I felt (federal prosecutors) did the best they could with what they had to work with, which wasn't much. The evidence just wasn't convincing. These were all government witnesses, and they were testifying both ways, in some cases admitting that certain physical evidence supported the defense's theory of the case as much as it did the prosecution's." (The jury had been instructed to avoid any news coverage of the siege in Waco, Texas, where David Koresh and as many as 80 of his followers were reduced to ashes when the compound was stormed by federal agents using heavy armor and set on fire.)

Bo Gritz was quick to speak up. "The message is: federal officials must abide by the law. In both cases, federal officials from the FBI and ATF agencies were persecuting people who merely believed in the Second Amendment right to bear arms. Somebody should stand trial. The federal government thinks they run things, and they don't. The federal mistake was in not following the law."

Weaver is viewed by many followers as a tragic victim of a runaway government that has the power to murder its own citizens with complete impunity. Many of these people believe that the only way to stop this is through armed aggression against the U.S. government.

Posse Comitatus

The Posse Comitatus is another Christian Identity group that proclaims whites to be the true descendants of the lost tribes of Israel, and that Jews, blacks, and other minorities have sprung up from Satan and are subhuman. Jewish bankers and the B'nai B'rith are spearheading the conspiracy directed against midwestern farmers.

Jim Wickstrom, a Wisconsin Posse leader and preacher, warns in his sermons, "The Jews who control the Federal Reserve control the availability of food." Denunciation of Zionism is standard doctrine. "Yahweh our father is at work setting the stage for the final act against the Christ-murdering Jews and their father, Satan."

In Kansas, a Posse-sponsored religious program aired to local farmers leaves little doubt as to the group's acceptance of violence as a way to bring about change: ". . . (The Bible) didn't say you're going to vote them out—it said, 'thus with violence shall that great city Babylon [that international communist system] be thrown down and shall be found no more. . . .' And all the disco bongo congo from the bongo is gonna be gone. All the nigger jive and the tootsie wootsie is going to go."

The Posse Comitatus was formed in Portland, Oregon, in 1969 by Henry L. Beach, a retired dry-cleaning businessman. Beach is said to have been an officer in the 1930s of the Silver Shirts during the 1930s, a neo-Nazi group that supported Hitler before the United States entered the war.

The Posse believes all politics are local, that the county sheriff is the highest legitimate elected official, and that the sheriff has the right to form a posse made up of citizens whenever the need arises. The Posse also believes that the federal government has far exceeded its limits as prescribed in the U.S. Constitution, that income tax is a violation of the Constitution, and that only the states—and not the federal government—have the right to declare martial law. According to a Posse bulletin, "The highest court in the land is the Justice of the Peace, which is closest to the people."

A 1976 FBI report estimated Posse membership at between 12,000 and 50,000 members, with many more than that considered to be sympathizers. There were 78 chapters in 23 states, with the strongest support centered in the Great Plains among the depressed farm areas.

In 1982, members of the Posse made the news when they grouped together and prevented a Wallace County, Kansas, sheriff from repossessing farm machinery. In 1983, a Posse member threatened to bomb a Johnson, Kansas, school unless the sheriff and undersheriff turned themselves in for execution.

In early 1983, a mob of Posse members in Springfield, Colorado, attempted to block the auctioning off of another Posse member's farm. And in that same year, in Medina, North Dakota, two federal marshals were killed during a bloody shoot-out with several Posse members led by Gordon Kahl, a decorated World War II combat veteran.

Kahl had done time in Leavenworth for income tax evasion and was then released on parole. One of the conditions of his parole was to stay away from other Posse members. He ignored this restriction and continued to roam the country warning of the Jewish conspiracy. This eventually caused the government to issue a retake warrant against him for violating the conditions of his parole. When they tried to arrest him in Medina, the shoot-out ensued. Kahl escaped but was gunned down months later in Arkansas by federal SWAT team members. Gordon Kahl was honored as a true martyr and American hero by the Posse. This helped perpetuate the movement.

Most of the Posse extremists refuse to pay income taxes or to maintain a driver's license or a birth certificate. This, they feel, reduces the government's control of them. They shun banks, preferring to stockpile and barter with silver, the common man's metal. They are fond of automatic weapons. They stockpile ammunition, food, and water in their homes and other safehouses. They keep in touch with each other through a variety of newsletters, such as the Upright Ostrich and the Liberty Lobby's Spotlight.

Today, the Posse's goal is to make the state wither away by raising children of the new generation that cannot be

Posse

BY LAW OF

Posse Comitatus

United States Citizens for Constitutional Rights

REDEEM THE REPUBLIC!

May 1981

In GOD We Trust

Posse Comitatus
Post Office Box 31
Evansville, WI 53536

U.S. CONSTITUTION

Posse Noose Report

Throughout the United States, State Police units are storing a tremendous amount of food stuffs and medicines. The main police post for each state also has a complete computer network installed with names of Christian Patriots therein, waiting for orders to unleash their forces against fellow Americans. This will be a direct act of TREASON against "We the People", and these forces must be totally incapacitated at that time. . . . Since the State Police are storing food (compliments of the American taxpayer), then SOMEONE has forewarned them of the trouble coming. Why hasn't Christian America been forewarned??

Disposable BODY BAGS are now being distributed throughout the states . . . There is no food being stored in Civil Defense shelters, but they have a BODY BAG for everyone. . . .

Other short notes: An old fort near Nevada, Missouri that was used to house German prisoners of war is being totally refurbished, including new fence and guard towers. This is one of many throughout the United States. Who does the Federal Government (KGB) plan to put in these human warehouses?? To coincide with this information, many county mental institutions are PREPARING their staffs with new medicines for a "new type of inmate who are not violent but do not like the present Administration in Washington . . ."

It is strongly suggested that ALL Christian Americans purchase at least nine months of food for EVERYONE in the family, munitions, guns, and other supplies . . . It is better to be prepared early than a day too late!! . . . The Posse is growing in ranks . . . The middleclass workers are striding with us, having found out why they are unemployed. The corrupt Jewish money and banking system that has bankrupted this Christian republic is the cause for the illegal foreclosures of their property. . . .

The "Cashless Society" (bank computers) is now interlocked from East to West Coast. Each business can be connected with their electric cash register through a telephone hookup to their local bank computer. . . . Isn't it nice how Rockefeller and his Jewish cohorts have made it so easy. Only one thing wrong—many people are waking up to the scheme and also to the constitutionality of LAWFUL MONEY versus PHONEY MONEY and the LAWS and RIGHTS of "We the People". "Hangin Tree, oh Hangin Tree. . . ."

I have been warning the residents of Wisconsin that a money problem was imminent . . . The Federal Reserve System is a private banking system . . . that manipulates the international gold and silver

Posse Noose Report.

standard in the world. . . . [It] is run and controlled by the Rockefellers and can create the recessions and depressions at will. . . .

Resolution #6, dated December 9, 1975, from Wood County, Wisconsin enabled the Conservation and Forestry Emergency Government to "establish an interim burial site on county owned land for use in mass county disasters." . . . "The Wood County Emergency Operations plan, as officially adopted by the County, requires provisions for an emergency mortuary service (bulldozers), which includes establishment of a temporary burial site for *mass casualty dead* . . . Recent reports have told of hundreds of thousands of people from urban locations that would be shipped north in an emergency.

Add it up:

1. Planned crisis by: monetary crisis through the banks, internal Jewish communist revolution, or limited Soviet nuclear attack upon major military installations and industrial cities.
2. Mass evacuation into preselected rural host areas. In the Civil Defense Preparedness Manual, Point #1 stresses no firearms permitted by evacuees.
3. Civil Defense Shelters have been emptied of food, medicines and other survival equipment.
4. Rural host areas have established mass burial sites. Massive amounts of disposable body bags have been distributed.

Please bear in mind that the Jews controlling our government on the local, state, and federal level, are selling the American people down the river.

Matt. 12:34-37
John 8:41-47
Luke 19:27

ARM EVERY AMERICAN
THERE ARE CRIMINALS ON THE LOOSE IN WASHINGTON

No man escapes when freedom fails.
The best men rot in filthy jails.
And those who cried, "Apease, apease,"
Are hanged by those they tried to please.

James P. Wickstrom

James P. Wickstrom
National Director of Counter-Insurgency

PASS ON TO A FRIEND

REPRINTED PERMISSION GRANTED

Posse Noose Report.

traced—children with no birth certificates who do not attend public schools and who grow up as true sovereigns under God and the American Constitution.

KU KLUX KLAN

First and foremost of the white supremacist groups is the Ku Klux Klan, founded in 1866. Many offshoots of the Klan have emerged over the years, such as the United Klans of America, Knights of the KKK, Invisible Empire, and California Knights. Some have long since faded into obscurity.

The Ku Klux Klan gained notoriety initially after the Civil War, operating as an outlaw army. It listed as the enemy Yankees, blacks, Jews, Catholics, and other minorities. Klan terrorists shrouded in mystery behind rituals, white robes, and hoods terrorized parts of the South for decades with their night rides and lynching of blacks.

During the 1960s, the Klan gathered support in its fight against the civil rights movement. Klan chapters opened in many northern and far western states. Other groups, borrowing from the Klan doctrine, preached bigotry to a new generation. In 1969, David Duke formed the White Youth Alliance (WYA) while enrolled at Louisiana State University. The WYA eventually became the National Alliance.

Duke, who went on to become a member of the Louisiana state legislature in 1989 and then toyed with the idea of running for president in 1992, fell out of favor with the Klan when he was suspected of being anything but sincere. Karl Hand, a national organizer of the Louisiana Knights of the KKK, accused Duke of ". . . conduct unbecoming a racist." Hand wrote, "The list here is almost endless, but let's leave it at this . . . don't leave your wife, your girlfriend, or your daughters alone with this guy. He has the morals of a Jew. This egomaniacal displays have cost Duke many a member. I can't tell you how many people used to call up KKK headquarters to complain about the Grand Wizard's behavior." Other allegations were made that questioned Duke's honesty and his violation of the Klan oath.

The logo and
emblem of the
Ku Klux Klan.

In 1980, Duke abandoned the Klan ship to found another all-white organization, the National Association for the Advancement of White People (NAAWP). Under his plan, the United States would be split up into sectors, each race being assigned to their particular area. He warned that without such a plan, the white race would be overrun by the nonwhite world.

In a 1983 NAAWP newsletter, he wrote: "Immigration . . . along with nonwhite birthrates, will make white people a minority totally vulnerable to the political, social, and economic will of blacks, Mexicans, Puerto Ricans, and Orientals. A social upheaval is now beginning to occur that will be the funeral dirge of the America we love. I shudder to contemplate the future under nonwhite occupation: rapes, murders, and robberies multiplied a hundred fold; illiteracy such as in Haiti; medicine such as in Mexico; and tyranny such as in Togoland. Am I an alarmist? Is my vision unreal? All one has to do is look around this globe and see the Third World reality. Are whites holding every one of the nonwhite countries down, or are we in fact pumping billions of dollars into them along with every technological aid that the West can produce? And now the West itself is gradually being enveloped by nonwhite immigration. The exploding numbers of nonwhites are slowly wrapping formerly white nations in a dark human cocoon. Shall a butterfly emerge, or a beast that has haunted the ruins of every great white civilization that submitted to invasion by immigration and racial miscegenation?"

PRIVATE MILITIAS

On April 19, 1995, the Alfred P. Murrah building, a multi-story federal building in downtown Oklahoma City, exploded with the force of a blockbuster bomb. Concrete and steel, glass shards, and human tissue rained down upon terrified Oklahomans blocks away. The toll of dead and injured was staggering. A tremendous 4,000-pound bomb had somehow been manufactured and delivered to a location next to the building and detonated. It was clearly an intentional act. Within a few days, the FBI had identified two suspects described as white American males and had arrested one. The media were quick to associate the two with the antitax, anti-government private militia movement. It was widely speculated that the bombing was planned in retaliation for the federal government's siege of the Branch Davidian complex in Waco, Texas, exactly two years prior.

Most of the militias are staffed by white men and women who have a paranoid fear of the government and of what they regard as the erosion and violation of their liberties. They view affirmative action programs and fair housing laws as a ploy by the government to suppress the accomplishments of white people. They believe the government is trying to teach white children to be ashamed of their heritage. These private militias have a military structure and a uniformed system of rank. They stockpile and practice with automatic weapons and other heavy weaponry, such as rockets and light artillery. They have their own intelligence net-

works, suppliers, medics, and communication experts. Bomb making is well understood by these groups.

Financing is shrouded in secrecy. Silent benefactors are suspected of supplying funds for these groups to equip their members with the latest technology in weaponry, communications, medical supplies, and other survivalist necessities.

Some of these private militia followers are curiosity seekers hitching a ride on a current wave of popularity. Others are sincere and hold strong beliefs. Some are recent arrivals, others have been around for many years. Most profess a belief in Christianity and an acceptance of Nazi ideology as it applies to Aryan supremacy.

WHITE SUPREMACY AND DEVIL WORSHIP

While many of the white supremacist groups incorporate Christian theology into their beliefs, others renounce Christianity and follow the teachings of the Satanists. The link here between Adolph Hitler's Third Reich and devil worship is inescapable.

Hitler's personal protective squad, the dreaded SS (Schutzstaffel) under the banner of Heinrich Himmler, copied heavily from the occult. The swastika, ritual dagger, lightning bolts, Runic SS, and death's head cap emblem, all symbols of the occult, stood out like a warning beacon when adorning the coal black uniform worn by the jackbooted Nazi elite.

Half a century later, the ghost of the Waffen-SS soldier would rise from the graveyards and arouse the youths, not only of modern Germany, but also of the United States, England, and other countries. In prisons, white inmates grouping together to withstand the threats of menacing blacks would adorn their bodies with tattoos of the swastika, Runic SS, lightning bolts, death's head emblems, and SWP (Supreme White Pride) in hopes of instilling fear into their adversaries, much the same as troops of the Waffen-SS had done decades earlier, when they caused antagonists of other European countries to recoil in terror at their approach.

However, these ragged, unshaven inmates now kicking

Death's head cap emblem.

rocks in prison are light years removed from the disciplined, relentless storm troopers of yesterday. When watching a line of disheveled inmates entering the culinary for the evening meal, devoid of personal pride or hygiene, an observer has to question the significance of the "White Pride" tattoo worn on the back of their upper arms.

Today's Satanists

Perverse sex, kidnapping, child pornography, excessive drug use, torture, and gang rapes are indulgences practiced by many satanists. Many of these practitioners wander across the country in "families." These nomads often engage in prostitution and "trick rolls"—a woman offers sex to a man in a bar or on the street and takes him to a motel or other ren-

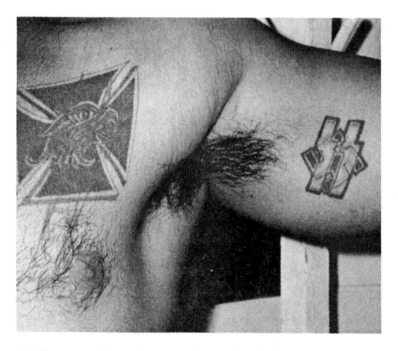

Nazi iron cross with eagle tattoo and swastika with Runic SS tattoo. These blunt-edged Ss are often mistaken for lightning bolts.

Tattoo of an eagle with "White Pride" on its wings and "SWP" on its chest.

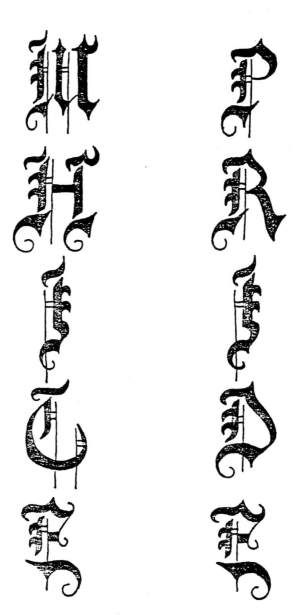

White supremacists often wear this "White Pride" tattoo on the back of their upper arms. "White" is tattooed on the left arm, and "Pride" is tattooed on the right arm.

dezvous, then her accomplices, usually one or more men, appear and rob him. During secret rituals, animals may serve as sexual or sacrificial objects. Tragically, infants are sometimes sacrificed. The more heinous the act, the greater the acceptance by the family.

Many teenage experimenters move toward satanic cults. As they become more deeply involved, they become subjected to various forms of mind control, including drugs, hypnosis, brainwashing, and trances induced by diet, sleep deprivation, and "cueing," a method of implanting subconscious suggestions into a person's mind that can be triggered at a later date to control behavior, which often leads to murder or suicide.

Anton LeVey, also known as the Black Pope, founder of the San Francisco-based Church of Satan, lists nine essential rules of conduct in *The Satanic Bible*:

· Satan represents indulgence instead of abstinence.
· Satan represents vital existence instead of spiritual dreams.
· Satan represents undefiled wisdom instead of hypocritical self-deceit.
· Satan represents kindness to those who deserve it instead of love wasted on ingrates.
· Satan represents vengeance instead of turning the other cheek.
· Satan represents responsibility to the responsible instead of concern for psychic vampires.
· Satan represents man as just another animal, sometimes better, more often worse than those who walk on all fours, who because of his "divine spiritual and intellectual development" has become the most vicious animal of all.
· Satan represents all of the so-called sins as they lead to physical, mental, or emotional gratification.
· Satan has been the best friend the church has ever had, as he has kept it in business all these years.

Satanic Cult Indicators

The following are some commonly found satanic cult identifiers.

- Altar containing candles, animal hair or parts, skulls, bones, knives, daggers, or a circle.
- Desecrated Christian symbols, such as an inverted cross or upside-down chalice. Other symbols may also appear inverted.
- Graffiti, religious figures portrayed as something sinister, drawings of pentagrams, devils, skulls, inverted crosses, flames, 666.
- Other Satanic symbols.

An altar showing evidence of burning and paintings drawn on the walls of an abandoned stamp mill near Virginia City, Nevada.

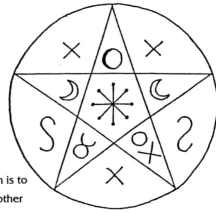

The circle has different meanings, one of which is to symbolize eternity. Another purpose is for protection from evil without and to contain power within. When used for ritual, the circle is nine feet in diameter.

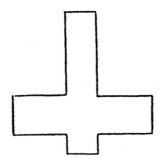

Inverted cross.

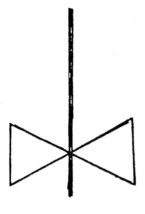

The Roman symbol of justice was a double-bladed ax in the upright position. The representation of "anti-justice" here is done by inverting the double-bladed ax.

Satanic writing over an altar found in the same abandoned stamp mill.

Depiction of a Satanic figure invoking a spell, also found in the abandoned stamp mill.

Pentagram.

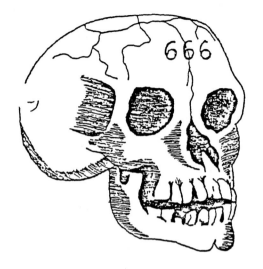

The mark of the beast may be seen as either 666 or FFF.

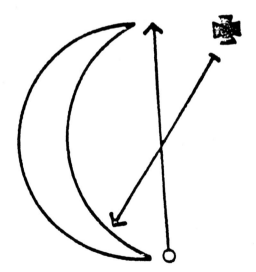

This blood ritual symbol represents human and animal sacrifices.

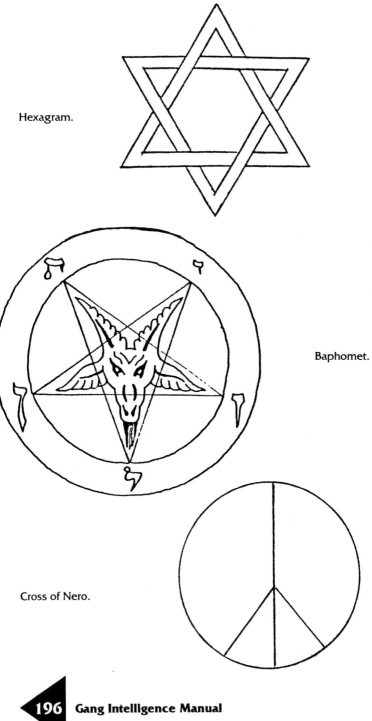

Hexagram.

Baphomet.

Cross of Nero.

Crescent moon and star.

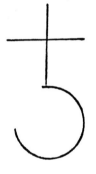

Cross of confusion.

Ankh.

THE RUNES OF ANDRED

A = ▽   N = ⊅
B = ⟊   O = ✕
C = ⌡   P = ⚏
D = ⌡   Q = □
E = Ŧ   R = ψ
F = ⌐   S = ε
G = ⟒   T = ↓
H = M   U = ∩
I = Ɏ   V = <
J = Ⴤ   W = ⋒
K = ✕   X = ℓ
L = ⇑   Y = ⇮
M = ⚄   Z = 3

The Runes of Andred.

The horned hand is a form of nonverbal communication between devil worshippers.

- Messages in Runic alphabet.
- The horned hand greeting.
- Robes, capes, hoods.
- Voodoo dolls, feces, incense, ashes.
- Animal body showing mutilations or carvings.
- Evidence of forced sex.
- Evidence of drug usage.
- Books: *The Book of Shadows*, *The Satanic Bible*, or *Magick in Theory and Practice* by Aleister Crowley.

YUPPIE STREET GANGS

Another phenomenon springing up around the United States is the social cliques made up primarily of white middle class and upper middle class youths that band together intent on disrupting society. These "yuppie gangs" have access to money, cars, liquor, drugs, and other indulgences. Many are in a state of rebellion against family and societal laws and derive delight from causing pain and suffering to others. Such a group has been identified by Las Vegas metropolitan police as the Shrikes.

Shrikes

The Shrikes deny their name comes from the shrike butcher-bird that impales its prey on thorns to eat at a later time, much the way a butcher suspends meat from hooks. They insist that the name comes from a character in a vampire movie.

In January 1993, the Shrikes were involved in a gang fight at a Spring Valley park involving as many as 60 combatants. Shrikes had assisted skinheads in the battle that sent three people to the hospital.

Then, in July, two former Clark High School football players, Matt Owens, 17, and Sean Ono, 18, both alleged Shrike members, were arrested and charged with murder after the fatal beating of Phillip "P.K." Shearer outside a Las Vegas Taco Bell on July 2. Shearer was slugged and slammed against a car, driven headfirst into a signpost, and left unconscious on the pavement. Shearer, who was to be a senior at Clark High, was declared dead on July 8, having never regained consciousness. Las Vegas Police Detective David Hatch said, "What makes this different is that instead of dealing with ghetto gangs, we're dealing with overprivileged kids that are mean-natured and enjoy hurting people."

Las Vegas Detective Tony Plew, a gang specialist, said of the Shrikes, "They don't appear to be white supremacists, but they do make up a hate group. Some of those involved with the Shrikes are minorities. They'll never go to the skinheads. Once you're recruited into the skinheads, you have to be of white origin. . . . The irony of the Shrikes is that some are being used so the skinheads can accommodate their own needs."

Plew said the problem of intolerance is spreading throughout Clark County. "Hate philosophies and hate mentalities are practiced by some students at Guinn and Cashman Junior High Schools. A hate group can be a bunch of kids that share a common prejudice, whether that's directed at one race or several races or certain groups."

Dan Reyes, acting chief for Clark County School District police, said the Shrikes have failed to stand out to officials who continually gather evidence about social groups that use street gang tactics. "There isn't any documentation on what the Shrikes do to indicate that they are organized or that their sole purpose is to victimize the public. They do exist, but as far as having an impression, we don't consider them a gang."

Reyes, who resists categorizing children as gang members, said school officials don't hesitate to intervene if a student's well-being is jeopardized by harmful activity. "The message is that students should report intimidation or threats. We don't have our heads in the sand."

OTHER WHITE GANGS

Roving street gangs are not limited to minorities. Whites in all parts of the United States are beginning to follow the path set by the blacks and Hispanics. During the past few years, Las Vegas metropolitan police have identified as many as 35 white gangs in the city. Gang unit officer Vince Hartung said in 1992, "White gangs are everywhere on every side of town. In Desert Shores you have the North Highland Boys, in the northeast area one of the gangs is the Stanley Street Bloods, but they're everywhere. There's a real ignorance among society as a whole. People think it's a black or Hispanic problem, but it's a community problem."

White gang members usually come from middle class to well-to-do families. Most have cars and plenty of spending money. Some band together for protection from the other gangs, others join "because it's the thing to do." Still others join for the easy access to drugs and the excitement.

Las Vegas police first became aware of white gangs in 1987, but the gangs didn't make headlines until two years later when Reet Boys member Michael Smith was charged and later convicted in the shooting deaths of Lino Abacahin and Jeffrey Randrup.

The shooting, which occurred near Bonanza High School just as students were leaving for the day, resulted from a confrontation between the Reet Boys and the Pinoy Boys, an Asian gang.

Louis Roberts, a Las Vegas police officer, said, "The Reet Boys started as a group of high school athletes who formed together for protection. They had a fight with a rival black gang and did well. From there it turned into a gang."

The Reet Boys continued to grow in membership, and other chapters were established. The Gold Bar Reets and the Green Valley Reets were two of these. The East Coast Bloods (ECB), which is one of the largest white gangs in the Las Vegas area with a membership estimated at over 100, was started by other Reets.

The Henderson Hood (HH) from Henderson, Nevada, is also said to number around 100 members.

As the white gangs increase in numbers and membership, they also enter into the rabid world of drive-by shootings and other forms of violence. After members of the East Coast Bloods shot it out with gang bangers from the Donna Street

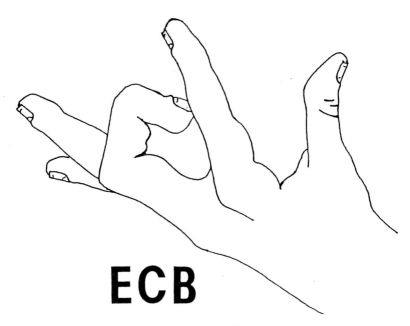

ECB

Hand sign used by the East Coast Bloods (ECB).

The HH in this tattoo stands for Henderson Hood, a white street gang in Henderson, Nevada.

Crips (a black gang) near the Italian American Club in Las Vegas, the police knew street gang violence had taken a nasty turn. One of the officers summed it up when he said, "They want to make a name for themselves. They don't have the mystique or the intimidation factor like the blacks or Hispanics do. And that's because of what the movies have portrayed and the ethnic stereotyping by society."

11 ▶ Prison Gangs

PRISON GANGS, IN ONE FORM OR ANOTHER, HAVE BEEN AROUND FOR decades. However, the organized, structured prison gangs of today are a relatively recent phenomenon, having developed during the 1960s and 1970s.

The gangs first formed along racial lines as a means of protection. As they matured, they went to war over control of the lucrative prison rackets: protection, extortion, mayhem, murder-for-hire, intimidation, prostitution, gambling, narcotics, and weapons manufacturing. Other less obvious rackets included control of inmate job assignments. For example, a captain's clerk is in a position to sell bed moves or confidential information regarding other prisoners, and the hospital porter has daily exposure to drugs, syringes, heating pads, and other amenities that make life more acceptable to prisoners. Many prison jobs have a good "pay number," which means that the job pays a salary in addition to giving "good days," days taken off the inmate's original sentence in exchange for work. In many prisons, tag plant (license plate factory) workers make top prison wages.

With very few exceptions, gangs within the prisons continue to form along racial lines, and their drug connections on the street are usually of the same ethnic background. The Black Guerrilla Family recruits only blacks, the Crips and Bloods are nearly all black, the White Pride groups recruit only whites, and Hispanic gangs recruit Hispanics but will accept others. The Mexican Mafia prefers Hispanics from the Southern California region; La Nuestra Familia prefers those from Northern California. Other groups that have yet to reach gang status are referred to as disruptive groups. In different prisons, these also form along racial or ethnic lines: Cuban Marielitos, Jamaican Posse members, Asians, Native Americans, blacks, and white neo-Nazi skinheads. Regardless of their status within the prison, they nevertheless recruit only their own kind. Some of these disruptive groups are extremely violent.

RECOGNIZED PRISON GANGS

In many states, illicit prison gangs have been established for decades. Others are born, evolve, and fade away, never gaining organization. Many prisons, as in California, identify and track these illicit groups and maintain files on all members. If the gang is of fairly long tenure, has identifiable leadership and solid structure, then it is classified as a viable prison gang. California's Folsom Prison recognizes five viable gangs:

1) Aryan Brotherhood: The AB is one of the most violent prison gangs and has strong chapters on the streets of many large cities. It has a long-standing alliance with the Mexican Mafia and has been at war with La Nuestra Familia and Black Guerrilla Family for many years.

2) Black Guerrilla Family: The BGF is the most violent and assaultive toward staff. It is very strong outside prison in California's Bay area and has an alliance with La Nuestra Familia.

3) Mexican Mafia: The Mexican Mafia may be the strongest prison gang. MM members attempt to run all prison rackets, including drugs, murder and mayhem, prostitution, weapons, extortion, and protection. They have strong ties

on the streets in Southern California and have an alliance with the Aryan Brotherhood. They have been at war with La Nuestra Familia for decades.

4) La Nuestra Familia: NF may be the most organized prison gang. Its structure is copied from the military. It has been at war with the Mexican Mafia for decades and has an alliance with the BGF.

5) Texas Syndicate (TS): The TS is a violent Hispanic prison gang made up mostly of Chicanos from Texas.

Aryan Brotherhood

An Aryan brother is without a care,
He walks where the weak and heartless won't dare,
And if by chance he should stumble and lose control,
His brothers will be there, to help reach his goal,
for a worthy brother, no need is too great,
He need not but ask, fulfillment's his fate.

For an Aryan brother, death holds no fear,
Vengeance will be his, through his brothers still here,
For the brotherhood means just what it implies,
A brother's a brother, till that brother dies,
And if he is loyal and never lost faith,
In each brother's heart, will always be a place.

So a brother am I and always will be,
Even after my life is taken from me,
I'll lie down content, knowing I stood,
Head held high, walking proud in the brotherhood.
—The Aryan Brotherhood Creed

The Aryan Brotherhood got its start in San Quentin in the 1960s. The gang, limited to Caucasians, came together as a means of protection from the nonwhite inmates. It was first known as the Diamond Tooth gang because the gang members imbedded diamond-shaped pieces of glass into their teeth. The name was later changed to the Bluebird gang, and all the members wore a tattoo of a bluebird on their necks.

The shamrock of the Aryan Brotherhood.

The gang at this time was fragmented and lacked leadership and purpose.

In 1968, hard-core members of the Bluebird gang joined with a handful of bikers and neo-Nazi groups and began to organize. They assumed more of a white supremacist stance, and the new gang was structured into a paramilitary type brotherhood with its own creed. They called this new group the Aryan Brotherhood. Their identifying tattoo—brand— was the three-leaf clover (shamrock) with the number 666 on the leaves and the letters AB beneath.

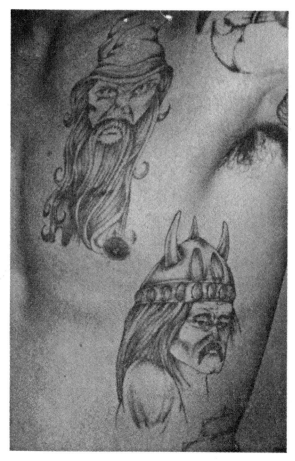

Tattoos with Nordic themes and horned helmets are popular with white supremacists.

Other tattoos reflected their white supremacist beliefs and have become a standard. These are mainly Nazi-style swastikas, eagles, bolts, iron crosses, horned helmets, and anything Nordic.

To be accepted into the gang, the prospect had to take a blood-in-and-blood-out oath, and the only way out was by death. But the hard-core members of the gang appreciated the security of being in a prison brotherhood and would willingly murder for the gang.

Shooter's Patch tattoo. This is an Aryan Brotherhood award, which signifies that the wearer has stabbed or killed while in prison.

The black and Hispanic gangs always relied on strength in numbers and had been recruiting vigorously. The AB approached from a different direction. They started by selecting a limited number of members on the basis of strength and willingness to kill. When the AB higher echelon issued a kill-on-sight order directed at its enemies, the whites went after the black inmates with a vengeance. Every morning when the San Quentin cell doors were racked open, the AB brothers stalked and attacked the blacks with the intent to kill. Anytime a Brother felt he had been disrespected, no matter how slight, immediate reprisal followed. It wasn't long before the Aryan Brotherhood had acquired the reputation of being the most violent prison gang.

The AB soon set out to gain control of extortion, murder-for-hire, prostitution, protection, narcotics, gambling, and other prison hustles. Wars against other prison gangs erupted over control of these illegal money-making rackets. In quest of their goals to control everything, the AB formed an alliance with the Mexican Mafia. These two emerging gangs became a formidable force inside the prison walls. They were soon responsible for a series of brutal assaults and murders and the introduction of greater quantities of drugs smuggled into the prison. Backed by increasing revenues, these two gangs were also responsible for the bribery and corruption of prison employees.

As AB members were released back into society, they hooked up to engage in street crime. They brought with them a history of extreme violence learned inside the joint and a devil-may-care approach to crime in the city. After all, they had survived in prison, had in fact lived fairly well, and few had any fear of returning. They were soon into underground drug and weapons trafficking on the streets, armed robbery, murder, and other violent activities. They maintained close contact with their Brothers still imprisoned and carefully tracked snitches and other enemies of the AB when these undesirables were discharged. Many of these former protective custody (PC) inmates were then hunted down and killed, some only days after breathing their first breath of free air in years.

AB gangs have started in other states, including Arizona and Texas, although it can't be stated with certainty that they are affiliated with the California Aryan Brotherhood. Some sources insist these out-of-state gangs have not been sanctioned by the AB, and that when any of these renegades are imprisoned in California, they must earn their bones again.

Prospective members of the AB must have a sponsor. After acceptance, the prospect is schooled by the Brotherhood. He must learn physical skills such as unarmed self-defense techniques, knife fighting, weapons manufacturing, baton takeaway techniques, escaping from handcuffs, key making, contraband concealment, sign language, codes, and a host of other skills needed inside prison walls. Also included are methods of compromising prison staff and instruction in manipulation of the classification process, in which the inmate may make several appearances before a committee to decide things like, which institution he will be sent to, where he will work, where he will go to school, if he qualifies for outside work programs, what his level of custody will be, and many other things. He is also expected to work out daily, lift weights, and stay in good physical shape.

The Federal Bureau of Prisons (BOP) considers the Aryan Brotherhood the most violent of the prison gangs within their system. The AB makes up less than 1 percent of the population but accounts for 18 percent of the homicides. As in the California system, the Aryan Brotherhood members in the BOP have an alliance with the Mexican Mafia to honor each other's hit lists and to share in the illicit prison rackets. In the Marion, Illinois, penitentiary, the AB has been responsible for a number of killings, including correctional officer murders, that have caused the maximum security prison to be placed on an extended period of lockdown.

Black Guerrilla Family

The Black Guerrilla Family is the oldest of the black prison gangs, having originated in San Quentin in 1966. Originally, the group was known as the Black Family and later the Black

Vanguard. It is the most revolutionary of the prison gangs and copies heavily from the writing and tactics of Mao Tse Tung. The expressed purpose of the organization is "power for the people."

The gang gained much notoriety during an aborted prison escape attempt on August 21, 1971. A lawyer visiting George Jackson, the founder of the gang, was accused of bringing in a gun and passing it off to Jackson during a legal visit. During the ensuing gun battle, Jackson was killed by San Quentin correctional officers. In the confrontation, three correctional officers and two other prisoners trying to escape with Jackson were killed. The attorney, Stephen Bingham, departed the prison prior to the escape attempt and hid out underground until 1984, when he surrendered to authorities.

In 1975, six inmates involved in the initial escape attempt were brought to trial on charges of assault, conspiracy, and murder. The trial was the longest on record at that time, not culminating until August 1976. In the end, three of the inmates were acquitted, and three were convicted. In the interim, a new leader had emerged to take the slain Jackson's place, James "Doc" Holiday. It is Holiday who changed the name from the Black Vanguard to the name it carries today, the Black Guerrilla Family.

Holiday had been active in the hierarchy of the Symbionese Liberation Army (SLA) and was closely associated with Bill and Emily Harris, leaders of the SLA. He had visions of bringing together other black revolutionary groups and creating a unified movement. After he was released from prison, he attempted to take charge of the BGF's illegal street crimes. It wasn't long before a power struggle developed between him and the leaders who were still imprisoned. In the end, many of the BGF gang members were gunned down.

According to California Department of Corrections officials, the BGF exists "to control the destiny of the black inmates, encourage cultural unity, and provide group protection." Although they have been a Marxist type revolutionary group, they move back and forth between revolutionary and criminal goals. Many of their members were once affiliated with the Black Liberation Army (BLA), a subversive group responsible for a number of murders of police officers in San Francisco and New York in the 1970s. Within the organization, there is a good deal of infighting and some power struggles from time to time.

The BGF has an alliance with La Nuestra Familia, and they work together in attempts to control the prison rackets and to carry out hits for each other. The criminal elements of the gang are involved in armored car heists, trafficking in drugs and weapons, witness intimidation, murder, protection, prostitution, and other street and prison activities.

The Mexican Mafia

"A member is to share all and everything. To have one leader or boss for all members and to swear their lives to the group with the understanding that death is the failure to comply with the codes of the group. Once an inmate is accepted into the group, he cannot drop out."
                                    —The Mexican Mafia Creed

The Mexican Mafia, or La Eme, has been recognized as an illicit prison gang for more than 30 years. Around 1957, at Duel Vocational Institute in Tracy, California, a number of young Hispanic inmates, street gang members from the Maravilla area of Los Angeles, hooked up together for protection against the black inmates. As more Los Angeles Hispanics came into the prison, they were recruited into the group. Soon, the street gang members from Los Angeles had attained sufficient membership to be able to cast aside the role of prey and to take on one of predator.

The group took the name La Mafia Mexicana. The members once again were caught up in the allure of gang membership, an allure they had not known since growing up on the mean streets of Los Angeles. The gang gave the members identity, status, and power over the weaker inmates. At first the gang preyed only upon black and white inmates, pressuring them for canteen items, sex, drugs, and money. They left the other Hispanics alone. But this soon changed. As the migrant farm workers from the fields of Central and Northern California entered prison, they became the primary targets of the Chicanos (Americans of Mexican heritage) from Los Angeles. The Mafia members looked down upon and

The eagle perched on a cactus killing a rattlesnake is taken from the Mexican flag and is the traditional tattoo and emblem of the Mexican Mafia.

despised the Mexicans. Their clothes were dirty, wrinkled, and oftentimes didn't fit. Their hair was unkempt and dirty. Many times the only belt they had was a string of torn up sheet. Few knew any English. They were illiterate wetbacks—*mojados*—and, as such, were less than human.

By 1958, the gang leaders considered other names for their organization, and finally decided on the name they carry to date, the Mexican Mafia, or La Eme for short. They are also known as the MM, and some of the more recent initiates spurn the traditional identifying tattoos and choose instead to wear a Mickey Mouse tattoo. This brand only hints at the MM, which serves to keep many hard-core gang bangers out of lockup during prison gang member sweeps. The Mickey Mouse tattoo is certainly much more subdued than the unmistakable and traditional tattoo of the Mexican Mafia, a snake and eagle.

During the 1970s, the Mexican Mafia engaged in total warfare against La Nuestra Familia. So much blood was shed that the California authorities inevitably moved the gangs to different prisons. Today, most of the hard-core Mexican Mafia gangsters are locked up in California's Pelican Bay, and most of the Nuestra Familia members are in Folsom.

The Mexican Mafia is heavily into street crime, including drug trafficking, weapons, and murder-for-hire, in the Southern California region. They allegedly have ties with Mexican drug lords in Baja, California, and Central America. They have also been able to hitch a ride on programs such as drug awareness and ethnic pride councils, all funded by the federal government.

In Los Angeles, on September 27, 1993, Mexican Mafia leaders warned Hispanic gang members on the streets to stop killing each other in street gang wars. They also emphasized that innocent people should not be cut down during senseless drive-bys. Hispanic gang bangers were warned that if they kept it up, they would pay a heavy price when they came to prison.

Since the warning, authorities said a 15 percent drop in Hispanic gang killings has resulted. Authorities are considering the possibility that the MM is making a concerted effort to unite all Hispanics to wage war against the blacks for control of the highly lucrative drug racket.

American Me

The movie *American Me* was released in February 1992 and depicts the life of an Hispanic youth from Los Angeles who is arrested for a series of crimes and then sent to prison. In the movie, his name is Santana. The real-life Santana was actually a prison inmate named Rudy "Cheyenne" Cadena. The movie portrayed some of the story correctly, but at times it deviated from the truth considerably.

In 1972, Cadena was stabbed 57 times and thrown off an upper cell block tier. The Hollywood legions, not caring much for truth, had Santana's friend Mundo doing the killing. In reality, the killing was ordered and carried out by the Nuestra Familia. The inmate who led the attack was "Tiny" Contreras. After killing Cadena, Contreras was moved to San Quentin and housed in very tight protective custody.

Another friend of Santana's in the movie was a one-legged inmate and friend from the street named J.D. J.D. in real life was Joe Morgan, who was one of the original leaders of the Mexican Mafia. Curiously, Morgan was not an Hispanic. He was of Hungarian heritage but had grown up in the barrio and had learned to speak Spanish.

During the filming of the movie, the star of the film, Edward James Olmos, along with other film personnel, traveled to the state prison to attempt to speak to Morgan. Morgan refused to be interviewed and sent word to the group that he considered their film wrong, and he made it clear that they would be "dealt with." The film makers must have taken the threat seriously because the producer of the film went into hiding for nearly three months.

Ramon "Mundo" Mendoza, a killer hidden out in the witness protection program, said scenes depicting the sodomy of one of the Mafia's founders and his impotence with women was too great an insult to allow. "Don't underestimate these people," Mendoza added. "If they're obsessed with getting to you, there's nothing you can do to stop it."

A prison inmate named Charles "Charlie Brown" Manriquez had been working as a paid advisor on the film. Manriquez was paroled from Pelican Bay State Prison on January 6, 1992. On March 6 of the same year, he was killed. Street talk blamed the Mexican Mafia.

On June 14, 1993, Ana Lizarraga, a Southern California gang counselor and paid consultant for the movie, was gunned down. She was the second person associated with the movie to be killed. Olmos, star of the film, said the murder of Ana Lizarraga was meant as a warning to him. He said he has also received death threats.

Lieutenant Leo Duarte, Chino Prison gang authority, said the gang members had been disrespected by several scenes in the movie. "This is their world, their environment. If they think you did something disrespectful, even if they're wrong, there's going to be repercussions," he said.

James Olmos, who has been trying to get a concealed weapons permit, said on the set of his latest movie *Roosters*, "These people don't tell you they're going to do it to you, man, they just murder. Trust me."

La Nuestra Familia

"If I go forward, follow me
If I hesitate, push me
If they kill me, avenge me
If I am a traitor, kill me."

La Nuestra Familia (NF), Spanish for "Our Family," has been a California prison gang since the early 1970s. Its founders and early recruits were, for the most part, farm workers and other disadvantaged people from the rural areas of Northern California. During the late 1960s, these itinerant farm workers were looked upon as sheep inside the prisons and were intimidated constantly by having their canteen items and other property stolen and by being assaulted repeatedly. They were despised by the U.S.-born inmates of Mexican heritage (Chicanos), who called them *farmeros* or *nesters*, and were regarded as something less than human by other prisoners of Mexican heritage.

The only protection these farmers had was to group together. As more entered the prison system, their numbers increased significantly. They began to fight back and made attempts to defy the predatory Hispanics, most of whom were affiliated with the Mexican Mafia.

On September 16, 1968, in San Quentin, an Eme member stole a pair of shoes from one of the *farmeros* and wore them openly on the yard as a challenge. After years of intimidation, this single act of disrespect was all that was needed to excite the *farmeros* into action. Tensions intensified, and a series of skirmishes ensued. The *farmeros* held secret meetings to lay out a plan for retaliation. During other secret meetings, the *farmeros* learned skills that were necessary for survival inside prison: self-defense, weapons manufacture, communications, and tactics of diversion.

In 1972, inside the California Institution for Men at Chino, the *farmeros* achieved their long-sought vengeance. Members of their group identified another Hispanic inmate as a leader of the Mexican Mafia. This prisoner was carefully tracked until he was caught alone and then unceremoniously murdered. Authorities moved quickly to stem the flow of expected violence. The *farmeros* who committed the murder were identified and moved north to Soledad prison in the northern part of the state. Here, they came together as a viable prison gang. At first they called themselves the Blooming Flower. This name did not seem appropriate, so they chose La Familia. Again they felt this name lacked something and then thought about using La Familia Mexicana. Finally, the name they carry to this day was decided upon: La Nuestra Familia—Our Family.

Originally, the gang accepted only Hispanics. This rule was later relaxed, and some nonHispanics have since been accepted. After the gang became established, it took on a structure with a chain of command much like the military. It relied on violence and iron-clad loyalty from its members. As the gang became increasingly structured, rigid standards of discipline were imposed upon its members. They were required to adhere to strict rules of dress, hygiene, and conduct. The gang copied heavily from the military, choosing to refer to the hard-core members as *soldados*—soldiers. The NF continued to grow, and as they grew, they expanded their criminal activities from the prisons to the streets of Northern California. Fresno was chosen as the home base, although regiments were established in many of the major cities.

In 1981, a federal gang task force was formed to stop the Nuestra Familia. Undercover agents infiltrated the NF, and 24-hour surveillance began. Informants and defectors were questioned repeatedly and then placed before grand juries. Afterwards, they were hidden out in the Witness Protection Program awaiting trial. After months of this intense scrutiny, armed with indictments and ample evidence, the Department of Justice went after the NF's higher echelon under the RICO—Racketeer Influenced and Corrupt Organization—statute.

By 1983, the structure of the Nuestra Familia had been seriously eroded. However, enough of the hard-core members remained, and they struggled to hold the gang together. Through this turmoil, two factions emerged. One faction, the most dominant, was led by a perceptive gangster named Robert "Black Bob" Vasquez. Vasquez was keenly aware that one of the reasons the feds had nearly destroyed the organization was because all of the gang members, including the lower echelon, knew the identity of all the leaders and the scope of the organization's criminal empire. This he recognized as a serious flaw that had to be corrected.

Vasquez's first priority in restructuring the gang was to establish three levels of rank within the organization. These he designated as Category I, II, and III. Gang members on Cat I would have no knowledge of the members residing on the higher levels. Those on Cat II would have no knowledge of those on Cat III. Only those gang members who had reached

Nuestra Familia tattoo.

Category III would have knowledge of the entire organization. A prospect entering the gang or a defector seeking readmittance would start at Category I and work his way upward.

As one progresses up through the ranks, he may become a member of an 11-man squad, or, if he shows leadership qualities, a squad leader. The rank of lieutenant is attainable for the *soldado* who has distinguished himself by making hits or by performing other meritorious service. La Nuestra Familia maintains a list of its 10 most wanted enemies, much like the FBI. The ranks of captain and general are within reach of the *soldado* who removes a name from the list.

The NF also needed a recruitment pool from which it could select its prospects. This pool needed to consist of proven street gang members and ex-convicts, preferably from the Northern California area, whose "papers" could be easily checked (prior street gang affiliation, criminal involvement, and possibly persons he has killed, which are attested to by other established gang members) and who would welcome the protection of a strong gang when they entered prison. The second faction from the Nuestra Familia, which was in the process of restructuring under the leadership of Robert "Babo" Sosa, was selected to become this recruitment pool.

This faction drew up a constitution called the 14 Bonds (taken from the 14 by-laws of the Norteño Manifesto), which became the rules the gang would live by. The name of this second faction became the Northern Structure. Members of this developing organization referred to themselves as Norteños, or Structure Brothers (Carnales de la Estructura Norteña). Later, some of the gang members sought out another name more in line with their Latino background. It was agreed that the gang would also be know as Nuestra Raza—Our Race.

Nuestra Familia Security

The Regimental Security Department (RSD) of La Nuestra Familia provides intelligence and security for the gang. This branch operates much the same way as any other security

department. The RSD maintains contacts outside of the prison whose job it is to compile and disseminate information. Wives and relatives of gang members are put to work in government offices such as the Department of Motor Vehicles, law enforcement, correctional institutions, and criminal justice agencies, including the courts. Public service companies such as telephone companies, utility companies, and other businesses that have personal knowledge of citizens often have Nuestra Familia sympathizers on their payroll. Their job is to gather intelligence on the enemies of the NF and to alert the gang to any impending crackdowns by DAs, judges, and law enforcement agencies. All information is compiled and stored on computer disk, retrievable when the need arises.

The security arm of the RSD teaches self-defense, conditioning, weaponry, killing techniques, interrogation, and related topics to the gang members. When they are released from prison, many have been schooled in methods of surveillance and countersurveillance. The instructors are chosen on the basis of loyalty to the gang, expertise in their fields, and the ability to teach. The students have a broad spectrum of learning, ranging from methods of making weapons from material available in the prison to communicating through the use of hand signing and code writing. A great deal of preparation is put into the schooling, and the students are obliged to learn.

Prospects for the gang are not just chosen at random. They must show their papers, and if deemed worthy of membership, they become a prospect. Next comes a background check done by the RSD that seeks to verify the number of hits the prospect has made, his past street gang affiliations, the status of his family on the streets, and other sensitive data. After the prospect is accepted, he is given a mission—usually an act of violence against someone who is considered to be an enemy of the NF. After the successful completion of his mission, he is placed on probation and sent to school.

Once he is initiated into the gang, the welfare of the gang—and not that of the individual—is foremost. The accepted gang member must now obey whatever orders he is given. Within the California prisons, NF *soldados* have been known to make a hit on someone they once considered a friend, and, in some instances, have even killed their own brothers. Enemy gang members have even been killed on the yard while being escorted by correctional officers and within range of the gun towers. Prospects on a mission have used the ploy of requesting protective custody in order to get into PC, where they could make the hit ordered by the NF.

Today's Nuestra Familia is engaged in drug trafficking, extortion, murder-for-hire, loan sharking, witness and jury intimidation, and other violent criminal activity, both inside and outside the prison walls. Despite the gang's emergence into computer sophistication, inmates not directly affiliated with them still refer to the NF gang members as *farmeros* or *nesters*.

Many years ago, La Nuestra Familia entered into a pact with the Black Guerrilla Family (BGF) for mutual benefit. These two prison gangs contract with each other to carry out hits, sell drugs and protection, and engage in other illicit activities.

Texas Syndicate (Sindicato Tejano)

The Texas Syndicate, or Te Ese, was formed in San Quentin in 1976 by Mexican-American inmates from Texas. The TS has far fewer members than does the NF or MM. However, they have a record of extreme violence within the California prisons and are now trying to branch out into illegal street crime in San Francisco and other Northern California towns. The gang admits only Latinos.

The TS gang members have distinctive tattoos depicting a subliminal T and S. A favorite is the depiction of an s with a larger T through it.

DISRUPTIVE GROUPS

If a group of prisoners shows little in the way of structure, tenure, and leadership, it is classified as a "disruptive group"

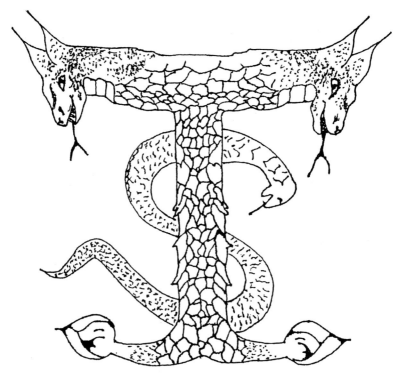

Texas Syndicate tattoo showing the large T through the S.

and not given gang status. Folsom, California, prison authorities recognize several illicit groups organized along racial lines that do not qualify as prison gangs. Some of these are:

1) Asian gangs: The Asians tend to remain together, but they do fight among themselves. The Pinoy Boys is only one of many of these Asian gangs.

2) Blood Line (BL): This gang may have been absorbed into the United Blood Nation.

3) Blue Note Crip Organization (BNCO).

4) Border Brothers: This gang is made up of Mexican nationals who have learned to gang up together.

5) Consolidated Crip Organization (CCO): This gang is attempting to unite all Crips.

6) Hoover Connect (HC): This is an emerging Crip gang. It may become more problematic than other Crip gangs. The HC will not accept certain Crip gang members into its organization.

7) Northern Structure: The NS serves mainly as a recruitment pool for La Nuestra Familia.

8) Samoans: These are South Sea islanders who tend to be big in stature and strong. They like to go one-on-one in fights. Some join Crips, others Bloods.

9) United Blood Nation (UBN): This is a highly structured emerging gang that is attempting to unite all Bloods under one umbrella. They tend to be nonconfrontational toward staff.

10) Wrecking Crews (WC): These are groups of violent white inmates, all of whom are all doing life or multiple life terms. They are said to contract hits and other acts of violence for prison gangs.

Northern Structure

Curiously, even though the majority of the Northern California street gangs claim to be Norteños and regard the Sureños as their enemies, many Norteño gangs are at war with each other on the streets. However, when these Norteño gang members enter the California prisons, they seek each other out and hook up under the umbrella of the Northern Structure. Members of the Northern Structure lay aside past problems from the streets and band together for protection against the other prison gangs, including other Hispanic gangs. The Northern Structure maintains close ties with one of the most violent Hispanic gangs, the Nuestra Familia.

Identification of Northern Structure Gang Members

Northern Structure gang members can be identified by the following characteristics.

- They regard all Hispanics from Southern California as enemies.
- They make liberal use of the five-point star (north star) in their graffiti, jewelry, etc.
- They identify with the fourteenth letter of the alphabet, N, and the Spanish equivalent, *ene*, or the words Norte, Norteño, Norte Califas, North Side, or NR (Nuestra Raza). A combination of Roman numerals and the letter R is seen as XIVR, which also translates into NR.
- They identify with the number 14. This may be written in several ways using both Arabic and Roman numerals: 14, X4, XIV, the Spanish *catorce*. Seen frequently in graffiti is a clock face with the hands pointing to the one and the four, and drawings often show the hands with one hand throwing up one finger, and the other hand showing four fingers.
- They identify with the color red.
- In prison, they are usually neat and clean and are nonconfrontational with staff.
- They may be heavily tattooed. The XIV is seen frequently in their tattoos.
- In prison, they are schooled in weapons manufacturing, self-defense and killing techniques, staff manipulation, methods of communication, and other covert skills.

PRISON GANG TATTOOS

If he has done much time in prison, the gang banger will probably have tattoos. Nearly all tattoos done in prison are very finely detailed and of blue ink only. Many inmates like to

In this Northern Structure cell wall drawing, the arrow on the gun tower is pointing to the north, the XIV and the word Norte are prominent, and the clock hands are pointing to one and four. Califas is written on the *vato's* headband, and the Spanish *ene* is near the Arabic number 14. Five-point stars are plentiful. At the extreme left, what looks like a backward L and a squared C are visible. This code writing is taken from a tic-tac-toe code which is used widely by prison inmates.

have the tattoos done on their arms, back, chest, and other areas that are readily visible. Large tattoos, which may cover the entire back or abdomen, can take months to complete. And if at any time during this period the work is brought to the attention of the administration, the inmate may end up in lockup. This does not apply to all prisons, though. There are some that allow tattooing as a means of better identification. Some, however, frown on the practice, citing the spread of contagious diseases transmitted through the needles, but it is doubtful that it will ever be stopped completely.

When inmates are caught with an illegal prison-made tattoo outfit, it is confiscated, and the inmate does some time in lockup. However, the inmates are quite willing to risk the sanctions in order to continue the practice. Tattoo guns are made from the small motors taken out of cassette players and a few other small parts. They are simple but quite efficient.

Tattoos are a means of expression. They are an indication of the wearer's thoughts. A heavily tattooed inmate can express his antisocial tendencies through his tattoos. One such tattoo is the anarchy symbol showing the letter "A" within a circle.

Many tattoos can be read like books if the observer has a fair amount of perception and training. The correctional gang investigator can appreciate the wealth of information available to him when he can read tattoos.

In prison, generally the more tattoos, the longer the wearer has been incarcerated. They are marks of pride or esteem to prisoners who have done a lot of time. Gang members like to show their gang name, hometown, and nickname. R.I.P. tattoos honoring their dead homies are popular. Spiders, webs, chains, barbed wire, gun towers, guns, and prison walls are seen in the tattoos of all inmates, regardless of race. The often seen teardrop below the eye or Pachuco cross on the web of the hand have no specific meaning; there are probably as many explanations for having these tattoos as there are persons wearing them.

This is a variation of the anarchy symbol tattoo, which is popular among prison inmates and other antisocial types.

Hispanic Prison Tattoos

Hispanic tattoos are usually of fine detail. They may show low rider cars, spider webs, *vatos*, bare-breasted women, their hometown *cliqua*, pistols, and shotguns.

White Prison Tattoos

Whites prefer Nazi symbols, dragons, snakes, spider webs, Nordic personalities, and Vikings in battle. Satanists sport the upside-down cross and other talismans.

Black Prison Tattoos

Tattoos of black inmates usually lack the detail and flair of the Hispanics' and whites' tattoos. Blacks like to show their nickname, gang name, and many times their enemies, i.e., CK (Crip Killa) or BK (Blood Killa). Dollar signs and Playboy bunnies are also seen frequently.

TIC-TAC-TOE CODE OF WRITING

Prison inmates have their own private grapevine. There are endless ways they communicate with each other, one of which is through code writing. One of the most often used written codes is the tic-tac-toe code. There are countless variations of this code. Page 232 shows the tic-tac-toe code used by the Nuestra Familia.

CASE STUDY:
GANGS IN THE NEVADA DEPARTMENT OF PRISONS

In 1985, the Nevada Department of Prisons was chosen for a special study by the U.S. Department of Justice, which was doing a report on prison gangs. Nevada was selected because of its lengthy history of violent gang activity. The Department of Justice was also interested in the success of the long-term lockdown status given to many of the gang members in Nevada. The two prominent gangs were the Black Warriors, who engaged in open aggression against other inmates and staff (attacking and stabbing three correctional officers during one encounter, and putting out a murder contract on the warden and associate warden), and the Aryan Warriors, who got along better with the staff than the blacks but had a history of extreme violence against other inmates.

The Aryan Warriors

During 1973, a troublesome white Nevada State Prison (NSP) inmate was sent to California on an interstate compact. While imprisoned in California, he was initiated into the Aryan

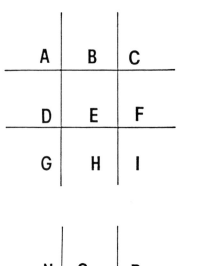

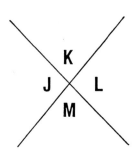

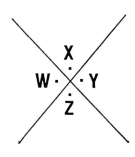

Example: N E V A D A

Written codes are one way prison gangs communicate with each other.
This is one of the tic-tac-toe codes of writing used by the Nuestra Familia.

Brotherhood. When he was returned to Nevada, he brought with him what he had learned about the creed, the structure, and the ideas of the Aryan Brotherhood prison gang.

At that time, the Nevada State Prison, a maximum security prison, had only a population of a few hundred. There were ongoing racial problems, and the housing was segregated. Many of the whites had been attacked by the blacks and were ready to listen to this inmate when he spoke of white rule in the prison and retaliation against the marauding blacks.

Several of the stronger inmates formed a white clique with the intention of starting an AB charter membership in Nevada. When the California ABs heard of this plan, they sent word that they refused to grant this charter and advised the Nevada inmates to form their own group.

The fledgling Nevada group held a series of conferences aimed at drawing up their own charter. Since they could not use the AB name, they decided on the name Aryan Warriors. The AWs thus started at NSP with somewhere between 20 and 30 members. The first year was disorderly as the group struggled for leadership and goals.

At the end of the first year, the gang showed signs of coming together. There was a recognized leader and a structure of rank was established: prospects, bolt holders, horn holders (council), and leader. Candidates were recruited from the yard; they were required to be white and preferably strong. They were expected to stand up to the blacks and come out ahead no matter what had to be done.

A prospect for the AWs had to be sponsored by one of the established gang members and be approved by a vote. The next step was to go on a mission, usually an act of violence against someone regarded as an enemy of the gang. Other targets were snitches and child molesters. After successful completion of the mission, the prospect was awarded membership and lightning bolts patterned after the Nazi bolts, which were tattooed inside the bearer's left biceps. A bolt holder was recognized as a soldier. He was expected to support his brothers at all times, and in turn he would be supported by them. If he were attacked by a black, his brothers would retaliate. If he were moved to lockup, they would send him canteen, tobacco, drugs, or other luxuries. If he needed a television, they would provide one. Camaraderie was high among the AWs. They addressed each other as "Brother."

The next step up in the organization was the horn holder. To become a horn holder, the bolt holder had to complete another mission, usually an act of extreme violence such as murder or grisly mayhem. A sense of leadership or special skills was also required. At the completion of this mission, another vote was taken, and if no one objected, the gang member became a horn holder. The identifying tattoo was a Viking helmet with horns and the letters AW on the front of the helmet. This brand was usually put on the left upper chest. A horn holder had much more status in the gang than the bolt holder and could be seated on the council. The council consisted of six horn holders and was seated directly under the leader. The council voted on all issues. The horn holder could also supervise the bolt holders and send them on missions not deemed serious enough to be voted on.

The AW members were required to pay dues. As the structure solidified and the gang's strength grew, they tried to take over most of the prison rackets, including drugs, extortion, gambling, loan sharking, prostitution, protection,

Lightning bolts of the Aryan Warriors.

and contraband weapons. The prevailing black gang, the Black Warriors, seethed with envy, and a showdown was inevitable. It took place in the culinary in 1976.

Prior to this event, the AW council held frequent meetings to decide how they could best discourage the blacks from the frequent attacks they launched on the weaker white inmates. In the end, it was decided that the blacks would have to be bloodied. They would attack them in the culinary during feeding. A secret powwow was held between the AW council and the leaders of the Tribe, a Native-American gang that was also having problems with the blacks. For the only time in the history of Nevada State Prison, a pact was made between the AWs and the Native Americans to attack the blacks together.

On the appointed day, the whites and Natives entered the culinary carrying concealed weapons. As though on cue, selected whites blocked the gas gun ports using food trays. And then the culinary exploded in a melee of prisoners intent on killing other prisoners. Officers, aware that they could expect no cover from the gas gun ports, fled the culinary. Shanks sliced the air and slammed into the unwary blacks. Clublike weapons shattered skulls. The blacks fought back, but when the riot abruptly ended, two blacks were dead and many others were injured. The AWs had accomplished their goals.

Aryan Warrior's horns.

In the ensuing weeks, suspects were gaffed up and put into lockup. Some of the Black Warriors made futile attempts at retaliation, but the whites had made a statement and were now the yard bosses. Many of the whites and Native Americans were eventually convicted of murder. But they were looked up to by their brothers as saviors, and the AWs grew stronger and marched ahead.

The Disintegration of the Aryan Warriors

The disintegration of the Aryan Warriors effectively began with the killing of Danny Jackson, a pathetically weak white inmate who was an informant, on November 5, 1980. What had once been the most feared gang in the Nevada State Prison was to become a crumbling structure as brother turned against brother in an effort to avoid prosecution for the murder. Ironically, some of the first gang members to roll over were the leaders that had ordered the killing.

Danny Jackson was a penny-ante crook, slight in stature and not of sound judgment. Prior to arriving at the maximum security prison in Carson City, he had been imprisoned at the Northern Nevada Correctional Center (NNCC), a medium security prison five miles away. He couldn't seem to keep out of trouble at NNCC and so was transferred to NSP where he was to meet his doom.

At NSP, he was immediately placed into protective custody because of a "snitch jacket" that had been placed on him. In PC, he whiled away the time telling lies and trying to scam the less sophisticated or "fish" inmates, who are usually open game for those who have been incarcerated for many years. His time was getting short—two months remained in his sentence—and the AWs wanted to get to him before he could leave. Messages were sent to him that all was forgiven and that he could come back to the yard. They probably enticed him with promises of drugs and other goodies. He contacted his counselor and insisted on being placed back into general population (GP).

The AWs were waiting with great anticipation—like stalk-

ing hyenas. The council appointed several youngsters to do the hit. On the destined day, Jackson was lured into the ancient bathroom located on the lower level of the cell house. This was a fine place to do a prison killing, because it had only one entrance and it was out of view of the guns on the cell house roof.

Inside the bathroom, he found himself encircled by several AW hopefuls, eager to earn their horns. He then realized what he had walked into, but it was too late. He was battered back and forth inside the circle until a noose was abruptly thrown over his head, cinched around his neck, and the other end tossed around the large pipe angled across the ceiling. He felt himself hoisted toward the ceiling, and then it was over.

The administration had been suffering under an umbrella of bad publicity the prison was receiving from the local media. The prison gang activity, killings, assaults, escape attempts, hostage taking, and other violent acts could no longer be tolerated. Top-notch investigators were called in, and the AW leaders saw the handwriting on the wall. Few of them wanted to pick up another murder beef, and soon snitches were lining up to testify. They did what many others before them and many others that came after them did— they rolled (made their own deal) and put the blame for the Danny Jackson killing on the youngsters.

The AWs who rolled were sent to NNCC in highly restrictive protective custody. A pattern emerged: at NSP, when a gang member thought he could make a deal, he let the officers know, who then contacted the attorney general (AG), who in turn made arrangements to interview him. After the interview, the inmate and his property were moved five miles away to NNCC and housed with a collection of other high-risk inmates, assorted snitches, baby rapers, and others who could not walk the yard in safety. But the AW rollovers were special; the Deputy AGs were going after murder convictions, and the testimony of these privileged Aryan Warriors would be critical to securing convictions. The AW rollovers soon realized this and began making demands upon the AG. They couldn't get along with this or that guard, they wanted ice cream brought in to them, pizza would also be nice, and how about a telephone. The demands taxed the patience of the officers assigned to keep them alive, who were caught in the age-old crisis—if the inmates weren't supplied with what they wanted, they called the AG, who in turn called the administrators. And it all rolled downhill.

Not all of the AW leaders ratted. Some hung tough. They were quickly identified, sometimes by the tattoos of the lightning bolts and Viking horns, but most often, and most reliably, by the other gang members that had rolled. They gave up everything, including the names of all members, who were sent straight to lockup. Many remained there for years. Still others were cast to the wind. Nevada had interstate compacts with most of the other western states in addition to prisons located as far away as Iowa and Connecticut. The Federal Bureau of Prisons agreed to take a few of the gang members considered to be the most dangerous.

In the end, three AW youngsters were found guilty of murder. They were each given additional life sentences. Some of the AW rollovers were released from prison early. Others, though, received little consideration from the pardons board or the parole board. More than 10 years after the trial, many of the gang leaders who testified are still in prison, still living in protective custody, despised by the general population, and subject to intimidation whenever escorted out of PC. They are referred to derisively as the Aryan Witnesses. One of the rollovers was set on fire while sleeping at NNCC. Most of the hard-core AW leaders had their tattoos—bolts and horns—covered up to avoid self-incrimination. They still have to look over their shoulders constantly and check the food trays given to them to ensure nobody has spit into them—or worse.

The Future of White Gangs

What we see today are various groups with little organization or structure. There are neo-Nazi groups, other SWP

(Supreme White Pride) groups, Satan worshippers, bikers, skinheads, a few Aryan Brotherhood members from different states, and other malcontent whites. There are a handful of white inmates from the Las Vegas area that were affiliated with street gangs before coming to prison. Some of these are known as Shrikes, Reet Boys, and Henderson Hood gang members. At best, these can be classified as disruptive groups.

At the Ely State Prison, a group called the Aryan Circle (AC) attempted to organize. They have one prison murder to their credit—a white inmate who had hooked up with a black. As had happened years earlier at NSP, three of the AC members rolled over and testified against the others. Two of the AC youngsters were convicted of murder.

The Aryan Warriors never regained their status within the Nevada State Prison system. White gangs in other states disavowed them because of the way they crumbled after the Jackson killing. Many of the former hard-core AW gang leaders that had been shipped out of state are now back in Nevada at the Ely State Prison. It may be that these AW leaders are attempting to restructure the AW once again into a viable prison gang. We have been told that the AC members have been given the ultimatum to either tip up with the AW or pay the consequences.

Black Warriors

Predictably, with the breakdown of the white supremacist Aryan Warrior gang, the white inmates on the yard were left with little protection from the black gang, the Black Warriors. Assaults against the whites by blacks increased. The whites were robbed, beaten, sexually assaulted, and forced to have money sent in, which was turned over to the blacks. Many were forced to have their visitors bring in drugs. Officer assaults were on the rise. The blacks held conferences and declared war against the custody staff.

One day, as three officers were escorting some black inmates to the lockdown units, the Black Warriors struck. The three officers were beaten and stabbed. Fortunately, they all survived. Two eventually were released from the hospital and returned to work. The other never again worked as a correctional officer.

Again the attorney general's office was called in. Black snitches lined up to tell, much as the whites had done earlier. The trial was heard in district court, where black inmates testified against black inmates. The suspects were found guilty and given additional sentences. Some were banished to lockup for years. Others were shipped out of state.

One good thing came out of all the turmoil—the breaking up of gangs. Gang members still in population quickly covered their brands with tattoos that were nonspecific. Nobody would admit to being a gang member. Occasionally, new groups poked their heads up to test the waters, but the AWs and the BWs had lost all credibility. The two most powerful gangs had been reduced to rubble.

The Future of Black Gangs

The majority of the black gang bangers at NSP are from north Las Vegas. Crip sets include Donna Street Crips, Rollin' 60s, Gerson Park Kingsmen, Bite The Dust Crips, Northtown Gangsters (NTG), and a number of others. Note that some Northtown sets also use an identifying number. Many of these Crip sets are at war with Bloods and other Crips in Las Vegas. Las Vegas Blood sets that are recognized at NSP are West Coast Bloods, Pirus, Hoods, Playboys, and United Blood Nation. When gang members from these Las Vegas sets come to prison, old hostilities are put on hold. Within the confines of the Nevada State Prison, all Las Vegas black gang bangers are expected to hook up together. The common enemy of Las Vegas black prison gangs is the 213 Posse—all Crips and Bloods from the Los Angeles area.

Blacks from Los Angeles that are doing time in Nevada include many from South Central. They have past ties with the West Boulevard Crips; Rollin' 40s, 50s, and 60s; Harlem 30 Crips; Five-Deuce Hoover Crips; Watts Varrio Grape; and many other Crip sets. Bloods are Inglewood Family Bloods,

Bounty Hunters, Swans, Fruit Town Pirus, Black P. Stones, and others. There are more problems between blacks from Las Vegas and blacks from Los Angeles than there are between Crips and Bloods at NSP. It is a matter of choosing sides based upon geographics rather than on color or gang loyalties.

There a few remnants of the Black Warriors left on the yard at NSP. These older prison gang members cause few problems—none that can be attributed to gang activity. Some of the youngsters coming into prison look upon them as worn out lames. The structure and discipline once associated with the BWs has faded, along with the black informants that testified in court against their brothers who assaulted the officers.

George Sumner, the administrator who effectively broke the backs of the gangs, slammed leaders in lockup for years and sent others to the "four corners"—various out-of-state prisons on interstate compacts. The few remaining at NSP who were caught up in those sweeps acknowledge that when Sumner rode into Dodge, it was all over.

At the present time, there are no organized, structured black gangs at NSP, although disruptive groups still prey on weaker inmates. Cell thefts are commonplace, as are attempts at protection and extortion. But the organized prison rackets and violence of the past are rare today. As long as the administration can continue to lock up those prisoners who try to organize, it will have the upper hand, at least among the white and black inmates. It may not be so simple with the Hispanics.

Hispanic Gangs

The Nevada State Prison has nothing that compares with the organized, disciplined Hispanic gangs that are prevalent in the California prison system. But the number of Hispanic inmates at NSP has increased dramatically in the past year or two. Many of these were associated with street gangs before coming to prison. They feel comfortable in a gang environment. When they enter prison, they tend to link up with others who share a common background and belief. In so doing, they accept the fact that they may be alienating others of their race that do not accept their principles.

Other Hispanics move away from the gang setting and consider it pointless to choose sides when both factions are of the same race. To them, the enemy could logically be inmates of a different color—or the prison staff. These inmates would like to bring everybody of their race together but not necessarily into a gang.

When a youngster arrives in the prison system for the first time, he goes through a period of indoctrination that lasts about three weeks. During this time, he is housed in the "fish tank," where he undergoes medical, dental, and psychological examinations. He is queried by staff workers, who attempt to come up with a fairly accurate profile of the prisoner. Where he will be sent to do his time depends upon such factors as his sentence structure, age, history, where his family lives, and many other considerations. During this three-week indoctrination, he will learn much more from the inmates than he will from the medical and psychiatric staff and the languid counselors that interview him. If he is an Hispanic, he will have been told what to expect when he hits the yard. At NSP, there are three distinct Hispanic groups (not yet well enough established to be referred to as gangs).

The Border Brothers

The Border Brothers, also known as Los Hermanos de la Frontera, or simply Los Mojados—The Wetbacks—are Hispanics from Mexico and other Central American countries. Many of them came to this country illegally; many others were green card holders when they were arrested. Few speak much English. In prison they are bound together by a common language, culture, and distrust of others. Many fear the presence of the white and black inmates. They fear the Chicanos even more.

Some feel intimidated by the correctional staff, because back in their country, uniformed officers were many times brutal, corrupt, and unpredictable. The Border Brothers are usually seen in groups speaking Spanish. For the most part, they avoid confrontations with staff.

Before coming to prison, many of the Border Brothers were affiliated with street gangs. Some of these gangs are Fresh Across the Border (FAB), 94th Avenue Locos (NFL), West Park Locos (WPL), Mexico Barrio Locos (MBL), and Barrio Mexico (BM) of California. Of course, there are many others. The Border Brothers claim the number 13, and many insist that their 13 pertains to Mexico, not Southern California. In Northern California, the Border Brothers have frequent wars with the Norteños (14). The *placas* of the Border Brothers are becoming much more widespread in the Northern California cities.

The Border Brothers lack the sophistication that the Chicanos have developed. Many have little schooling or skills. They are looked down upon by the Hispanics born in this country. This has led to recurrent confrontations, both in the prison system and on the streets where frequent gunfights erupt, most noticeably in Northern California cities such as Oakland, San Francisco, and cities in the farm belt like Stockton.

Some general characteristics of Border Brothers gang members are as follows.

- The Border Brothers are fewer in number throughout the prison system in relation to the other Hispanics.
- They are usually seen in groups.
- They identify with the color black.
- Border Brothers leaders may have excellent drug connections in Mexico and Columbia. Besides marijuana and cocaine, the Mexicans are getting very involved with the manufacture and distribution of methamphetamine.
- The Border Brothers regard the Hispanics born in this country (Chicanos) as hypocrites.
- Many Border Brothers dress like the *campesinos* in Mexico—careless—and clothing may be ragged and

unclean. A belt, if worn, may be nothing more than a piece torn from a bed sheet.

- They enjoy playing handball, horseshoes, and soccer.
- Tattoos are popular. The name of their home state in Mexico may be displayed across their back, abdomen, or chest, as may their name. Depictions of Pancho Villa wearing cartridge bandoleers are seen frequently across their chests, as are religious figures, gang names, and the number 13.
- The Border Brothers don't have to recruit. When a Mexican national shows up at the prison, he will naturally gravitate toward those he feels comfortable with.

Sinaloan Cowboys

The Sinaloan Cowboys are Mexican nationals from the states of Sinaloa, Chihuahua, Durango, Michoacan, Nayarit, and Zacatecas. These gangsters have a long-standing history of structured gang activity in their home states. On the streets of California, they have become extremely violence prone. They are heavily involved in narcotics trafficking, homicides, and assaults against police. They are being tracked closely within the Nevada prison system.

Following are some identifying characteristics of Sinaloan Cowboy gang members.

- Their emblem is a rope lasso supporting a saddle. Brahma bulls are also seen frequently.
- They like to wear expensive gold jewelry.
- They are well groomed.
- On the streets of Southern California, they have working relationships with Hispanic gangs to sell their drugs and commit other crimes for pay.

Mi Raza Unida and Los Aguilas

At NSP, a group of inmates, many of whom are in lockup, refer to themselves as members of Mi Raza Unida (MRU, My United Race) or Los Aguilas (The Eagles).

The MRU have a distinctive emblem that they use fre-

quently in their graffiti, literature, and tattoos, taken from the Mexican flag: an eagle perched on a cactus clutching a snake between its beak and claw.

This eagle representation is nearly identical to one used by the Mexican Mafia in California. The MM has taken offense at this use of its emblem by the Nevada Hispanics. Even so, the Nevada group has been trying to get a chapter sanctioned by the MM. To this date, the MM have refused to grant this.

The Aguilas at NSP have the most potential for organizing. The hard-core members have been involved in numerous assaults, including an organized ambush against a few Norteños. They demonstrate a high degree of loyalty toward one another and despise the Border Brothers and Norteños. In lockup, they have become troublesome on occasion, and it has been necessary for the officers to use force against them.

The Aguilas regard themselves as Americans—which they are—yet they pride themselves on the color of their skin. Many have "Brown Pride" or "*Orgullo Mexicano*" (Mexican Pride) tattooed on the back of their upper arms. Most speak very good English, and many speak little or no Spanish.

Following are some general characteristics of these gang members.

- They have great loyalty toward each other. They willingly share canteen and other luxuries.
- Most are fluent in English.
- They identify with Sureño, the number 13, and the color blue.
- Most Aguilas are neat, well groomed, and wear razor creased trousers. Their shoes may have a high shine.
- Their gang emblem, the eagle and snake, is taken from the Mexican flag.
- They may be heavily tattooed. Their street *cliqua*, nickname, and *vato* or low rider type tattoos are preferred. The identifying 13, Sur, and Sureño are seen regularly.
- Their hair is usually worn short or shaved, but they may

Tattoo of Los Aguilas showing an eagle perched on a cactus and clutching a rattlesnake in its beak and claw. This emblem was taken from the Mexican flag.

have a tail. Other than a mustache, they are usually clean shaven.

- They enjoy handball, basketball, and weight lifting.
- They regard all northern Hispanics—Norteños—as enemies.
- The Aguilas recruit actively. When a new Chicano hits the yard, the Aguilas immediately determine if he claims Sureño. If so, he is welcomed.

Northern Structure

Already well established in California, Northern Structure gang members are being seen more frequently in the Nevada prison system.

They clique up together, work out together, and generally avoid confrontations with correctional staff. Northern Structure gangs maintain strong contacts with other Norteño gangs, including the Nuestra Familia in Northern California.

Some identifying characteristics of Northern Structure gang members are as follows.

- They are usually neat and clean shaven. Their shoes may have a high shine. They work out together and move around the yard in a small group.
- They identify with the color red.
- Many are heavily tattooed. They identify with the number 14, and this is seen in their tattoos, graffiti, and literature.
- Recruitment is limited to those gang bangers from Northern California.
- The Structure Brothers are generally respectful toward staff.
- They maintain strong ties on the streets of Northern California and may also have affiliations with the powerful Nuestra Familia.

This graffiti is a good example of Northern Structure art. The artist's hometown (Hayward) is shown at the top of the piece. The N and R stand for Nuestra Raza—Our Race. On the upturned brim of the sombrero is the inscription "Calle XIVER" and the letter N. This translates to "Nuestra Raza Street." The figure poking out from behind the bars is throwing up a one and a four using his fingers, another reference to the number 14. The name of the artist is shown at the left of the figure, Mano, and his partner's name, Indio, is shown to the right of the figure. The N.S.L.S. stands for Northern Structure Locos.